Building SPELLING Skills

Grade 4

Daily Practice

What's in This Book?

This 30-unit book contains strategies and practice for learning 540 spelling words.

Each unit contains:

- a list of 18 spelling words
- two sentences for dictation
- four activity pages for practicing the spelling words

Words on the spelling lists were selected from:

- a list of the 400 most commonly used words in English
- words frequently misspelled by fourth-graders
- words with common phonetic elements
- words changed by adding prefixes and suffixes and by forming compound words and contractions.

Additional resources:

- "How to Study" chart
- "Spelling Strategies" chart
- forms for testing and recordkeeping

Correlated to State Standards

Visit *www.teaching-standards.com* to view a correlation of this book's activities to your state's standards. This is a free service.

EMC 2708

Evan-Moor®
EDUCATIONAL PUBLISHERS
Helping Children Learn since 1979

Authors: Doug and Sharman Wurst
Editor: Leslie Sorg
Copy Editor: Cathy Harber
Illustrator: Jim Palmer
Desktop: Jia-Fang Eubanks
             Yuki Meyer

Contents

Week	Focus
14	
15	
16	
17	
18	
19	
20	
21	
22	
23	
24	
25	
26	
27	
28	
29	
30	

Teaching the Weekly Unit

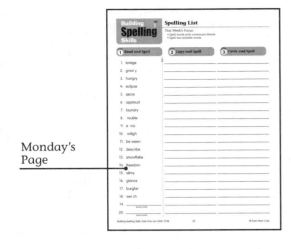

Monday's Page

Monday

Allot ample class time each Monday for introducing the spelling list and having students complete the first page of the unit.

Introducing the Week's Words

Give each student the spelling list for the week. Here are ways to introduce the words:

- Call attention to important consistencies noted in "This Week's Focus," such as a phonetic or structural element. For example, say: *As we read this week's spelling list, notice that all the words have the same vowel sound.*
- Read each word aloud and have students repeat it.
- Provide a model sentence using the word. Have several students give their own sentences.
- If desired, add "bonus words" based on the needs of your class. These may be high-utility words or words that the class is encountering in curricular studies.

Writing the Words

After introducing the words, have students study and write the words on the first page of the unit, following these steps:

Step 1: Read and Spell
Have students read the word and spell it aloud.

Step 2: Copy and Spell
Tell students to copy the word onto the first blank line and spell it again, touching each letter as it is spoken.

Step 3: Cover and Spell
Have students fold the paper along the fold line to cover the spelling words so that only the last column shows. Then have students write the word from memory.

Step 4: Uncover and Check
Tell students to open the paper and check the spelling. Students should touch each letter of the word as they spell it aloud.

Home Connection

Send home a copy of the Parent Letter (page 145) and the Take-Home Spelling List for the week (pages 10–19).

Strengthening Students' Spelling Skills

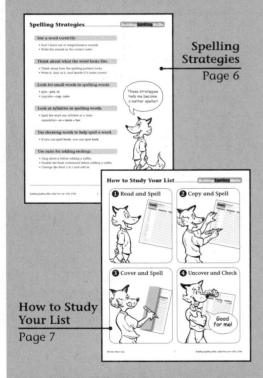

Spelling Strategies
Page 6

How to Study Your List
Page 7

At the beginning of the year, reproduce pages 6 and 7 for each student or on an overhead transparency. Review the general steps and strategies, encouraging students to apply them throughout the year.

Tuesday — Word Meaning and Dictation

Have students complete the Word Meaning activity on the second page of the unit. Then use the dictation sentences on pages 8 and 9 to guide students through "My Spelling Dictation." Follow these steps:

1. Ask students to listen to the complete sentence as you read it.

2. Say the sentence in phrases, repeating each phrase one time clearly. Have students repeat the phrase.

3. Wait as students write the phrase.

4. When the whole sentence has been written, read it again, having students touch each word as you say it.

Wednesday — Word Study Activities

Have students complete the activities on the third page of the unit. Depending on students' abilities, these activities may be completed as a group or independently.

Thursday — Edit for Spelling Activities

Have students complete the activities on the fourth page. Depending on students' abilities, these activities may be completed as a group or independently.

Friday — Weekly Test

Friday provides students the chance to take the final test and to retake the dictation they did on Tuesday. A reproducible test form is provided on page 142. After the test, students can record their score on the "My Spelling Record" form (page 141).

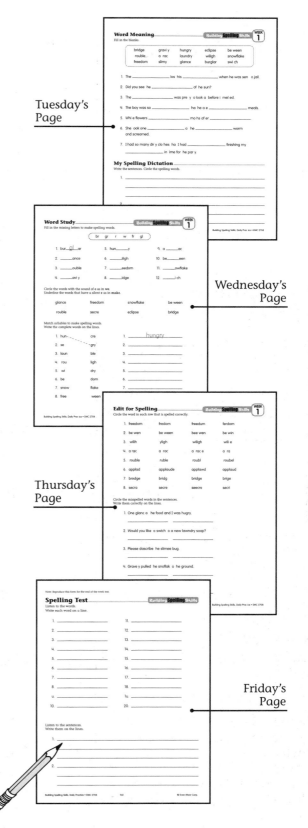

Tuesday's Page

Wednesday's Page

Thursday's Page

Friday's Page

Spelling Strategies

Say a word correctly.

- Don't leave out or mispronounce sounds.
- Write the sounds in the correct order.

Think about what the word looks like.

- Think about how the spelling pattern looks.
- Write it, look at it, and decide if it looks correct.

Look for small words in spelling words.

- spin—**pin**, **in**
- cupcake—**cup**, **cake**

Look at syllables in spelling words.

- Spell the word one syllable at a time.
  remember—**re • mem • ber**

These strategies help me become a better speller!

Use rhyming words to help spell a word.

- If you can spell **book**, you can spell **look**.

Use rules for adding endings.

- Drop silent **e** before adding a suffix.
- Double the final consonant before adding a suffix.
- Change the final **y** to **i** and add **es**.

How to Study Your List

❶ Read and Spell

❷ Copy and Spell

❸ Cover and Spell

❹ Uncover and Check

Good for me!

Sentences for Dictation

There are two dictation sentences for each spelling list. Space for sentence dictation is provided on Tuesday of each week and on Friday's test form (page 142).

- Ask students to listen to the complete sentence as you read it.
- Have students repeat the sentence.
- Read the sentence in phrases, repeating each phrase one time clearly.
- Have students repeat the phrase.
- Allow time for students to write the phrase.
- Read the sentence again, having students touch each word as you say it.

Week   Dictation Sentences

1   Was there **trouble between** the two **laundry** workers?
   We stood on the **bridge** to **glance** at the **eclipse**.

2   The **thirsty athlete** drank **spring** water to wet his **whistle**.
   Is that **sandwich worth** what you paid?

3   My **neighbor** was carrying **freight** when his **ankle began** to twist.
   Please **explain** why the **main display** will end in **April**.

4   The girl was **eager** to **receive** her lost **sneakers**.
   I **believe** it is not **easy** for **people** to **squeeze** juice from oranges.

5   **Which bicycle** is the **right** one to **buy**?
   Did he **decide** to **write** a story about **lightning** hitting a **skyscraper**?

6   I had no **control** when I saw the **doughnuts** in the **bowl**.
   Was it **wrong** to **copy** the **problem shown** in the book?

7   My **uncle** wears a **used uniform** when he works as an **umpire**.
   Is it **usual** to **blush** when someone says you are **beautiful**?

8   All the **dollars** in his **wallet** won't buy a **million scissors**.
   Follow this map to find the **address** of the **office**.

9   The **calendar** says that school starts the first **Wednesday** in **September**.
   Is **autumn** the **season** of the **year** you like best?

10   I asked my **brother** to **purchase** a **banana** for me.
   My **cousin** uses a **compass** to sail **across** the **ocean**.

11   **I'm** sure **you'll** be the one **who's** next.
   They **could've** asked for me, but **you're** the one **they'd** like.

12   Did he go **downstairs** to have **breakfast** with his **grandparents**?
   Anyone would be surprised to find a **scarecrow** in the **outfield**.

13   I was **hoping** we would be **studying living** things.
   It **appeared** that he was **changing** the **wrapping** on the gift.

Week Dictation Sentences

14 Was the **busiest** dog **happier** than the **laziest** dog?
The **biggest** and **heaviest** rock also has the **roughest** feel.

15 The **barber** cut the **sailor's curly** hair **early** in the morning.
I **wonder** if the **service** is **worse** at the **bakery** or at the flower shop.

16 Will you eat one **potato** or two **potatoes**?
Their **journeys** took the **family** through a **ditch** full of **leaves**.

17 Use **caution because** the **faucet** is leaking water.
The **lawyer** would **cough** when a **false** statement was given.

18 A loud **concert** is **dangerous** and may **damage** your hearing.
Did you see the **cardinal circle** the **ledge**?

19 Is there any **news** about **who ruined** the **schoolroom**?
Whose duty is it to tell the **truth** to Julie?

20 Please **avoid** getting **moisture** in the **thousand** sacks of **flour**.
Do you **enjoy** making a large **amount** of **noise** to **annoy** me?

21 My **nephew** told me the **alphabet** over the **telephone**.
Did you write a **paragraph** about the **giraffe** that won a **trophy**?

22 My **daughter ought** to use a **brighter flashlight**.
The **naughty** child was at **fault** for the **nightly** mess in the kitchen.

23 The **calf walked** to the door and **gnawed** on the **wreath**.
Did the **climber fasten** the rope to his **wrist**?

24 I'm on a **mission** to **educate** students about the problems of **pollution**.
Does the **musician's expression express** her feeling about the **music**?

25 The **pilot** saw the **gigantic volcano** erupt.
Is this **climate really** to your liking?

26 I **heard** a **herd** of cattle heading **straight** for the **strait**.
Their ceiling needed **sealing** over **there**.

27 The **angel** was **quite quiet**.
Did a **loose** pitch cause the **pitch**er to **lose** the game?

28 The **tireless** volunteer was **hopeful** that she could help the **homeless** family.
Did the **friendly** teacher show **goodness** and **kindness** toward the **fearful** student?

29 I always **disappoint** myself when I am **unkind** or **dishonest**.
I'm **uncomfortable** when we **disagree** about how to **rewrite** the report.

30 The **experiment** needed a very low **temperature** for the **oxygen** to freeze.
There was a lively **discussion** about everyone's **favorite computer**.

bridge

gravity

hungry

eclipse

secret

applaud

laundry

trouble

attract

twilight

between

describe

snowflake

freedom

slimy

glance

burglar

switch

bonus word

bonus word

cut

attach

where

sandwich

change

watch

singer

slippery

spring

gather

these

thread

athlete

worth

thirsty

whisper

whistle

awhile

nowhere

bonus word

bonus word

cut

fact

began

clasp

rapid

able

later

space

stranger

grade

display

main

explain

freight

neighbor

weigh

vein

April

ankle

bonus word

bonus word

then	since	strong
else	which	wrong
edge	inch	copy
when	string	cloth
tenth	picnic	problem
empty	shrimp	bottom
sketch	title	whole
spelling	mind	explode
easy	wild	control
eager	decide	shown
sneakers	why	bowl
mean	skyscraper	October
fifteen	buy	smoky
receive	right	coach
piece	lightning	throat
believe	write	toast
people	cypress	doughnut
squeeze	bicycle	foe

cut

cut

bonus word

bonus word

bonus word

bonus word

bonus word

bonus word

blush	follow	Tuesday
crutch	matter	Wednesday
crunch	summer	Thursday
grumpy	million	Saturday
much	dollar	January
umpire	scissors	February
uncle	cattle	July
none	address	August
does	office	September
fuel	suppertime	November
cute	blizzard	month
cubicle	penny	year
human	wrapper	holiday
future	wallet	autumn
usual	occurrence	season
uniform	village	calendar
used	collide	second
beautiful	battle	minute

cut

cut

_____

bonus word

_____

bonus word

_____

bonus word

_____

bonus word

_____

bonus word

_____

bonus word

across

alone

among

brother

again

front

banana

appear

compass

pedal

given

heaven

mountain

ocean

cousin

purchase

often

color

_____
bonus word

_____
bonus word

didn't

that's

they're

you're

couldn't

haven't

o'clock

we're

isn't

I'm

it's

who's

they'd

could've

they've

you'll

don't

aren't

_____
bonus word

_____
bonus word

cut

anyone

however

everything

himself

birthday

herself

somewhere

afternoon

chalkboard

daydream

downstairs

grandparents

breakfast

outfield

scarecrow

nobody

dragonfly

keyboard

_____
bonus word

_____
bonus word

cut

lived	cleaner	early
living	cleanest	earth
rattled	bigger	search
rattling	biggest	service
studied	earlier	wonder
studying	earliest	surface
traveled	quicker	curly
traveling	quickest	shirt
changed	busier	thirty
changing	busiest	doctor
appeared	rougher	sailor
appearing	roughest	shower
raced	heavier	bakery
racing	heaviest	another
hoped	happier	barber
hoping	happiest	collar
wrapped	lazier	worse
wrapping	laziest	world

cut

cut

_____

bonus word

_____

bonus word

_____

bonus word

_____

bonus word

_____

bonus word

_____

bonus word

Week 16	Week 17	Week 18
leaf	also	cinder
leaves	bought	circle
wolf	cough	cardinal
wolves	almost	cereal
potato	false	cycle
potatoes	officer	concert
roof	soft	dancer
roofs	stalk	celebrate
family	halt	twice
families	faucet	dangerous
library	saucer	strange
libraries	caution	ledge
journey	lawyer	damage
journeys	awesome	geography
hero	stall	gentle
heroes	crawl	signal
ditch	awful	regular
ditches	because	sugar

cut

cut

_____
bonus word

_____
bonus word

_____
bonus word

_____
bonus word

_____
bonus word

_____
bonus word

Week 19	Week 20	Week 21
shoes	voice	enough
clues	oyster	tougher
wound	voyage	fifty
junior	annoy	pharmacy
truth	choice	alphabet
duty	avoid	nephew
news	appoint	trophy
through	enjoy	paragraph
few	moisture	telephone
who	noise	photograph
schoolroom	drown	giraffe
whose	amount	forest
conclusion	fountain	figure
June	crowded	refrigerator
shampoo	southwest	draft
cruel	thousand	phrase
choose	flour	traffic
ruin	pronounce	chief

cut

cut

_____
bonus word

_____
bonus word

_____
bonus word

_____
bonus word

_____
bonus word

_____
bonus word

frighten	calf	action
flight	walked	fiction
brighter	ghost	mission
flashlight	gnawed	divide
mighty	climber	division
delight	wreath	attend
tighten	listen	attention
nightly	island	pollute
sight	scent	pollution
brought	wrench	express
ought	judge	expression
thought	fasten	educate
fought	wrist	education
caught	doubt	music
daughter	knock	musician
taught	answer	magic
naughty	knelt	magician
fault	sign	physician

cut

cut

_____
bonus word

_____
bonus word

_____
bonus word

_____
bonus word

_____
bonus word

_____
bonus word

Building Spelling Skills

NAME   WEEK
                        25

Building Spelling Skills

NAME   WEEK
                        26

Building Spelling Skills

NAME   WEEK
                        27

Week 25	Week 26	Week 27
lazy	herd	quiet
volcano	heard	quite
flavor	clothes	angel
piano	close	angle
recent	hour	already
really	our	all ready
item	two	desert
pilot	too	dessert
triangle	their	weather
climate	there	whether
gigantic	ceiling	pitcher
program	sealing	picture
obey	shoot	loose
puny	chute	lose
prepare	strait	aisle
vacant	straight	isle
pulley	medal	dairy
menu	meddle	diary

_____
bonus word

_____
bonus word

_____
bonus word

_____
bonus word

_____
bonus word

_____
bonus word

cut

cut

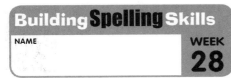

Week 28

hopeless

careless

homeless

tireless

hopeful

fearful

cheerful

careful

graceful

happily

friendly

angrily

swiftly

suddenly

darkness

goodness

sadness

kindness

_____
bonus word

_____
bonus word

Week 29

disappear

disappoint

disagree

dishonest

unable

uncertain

unbeaten

uncomfortable

unkind

unknown

rewrite

review

rebuild

recall

misbehave

misuse

misunderstand

misspell

_____
bonus word

_____
bonus word

Week 30

multiply

imagination

favorite

computer

citizenship

invisible

undercover

enjoyment

discussion

America

unusual

example

melody

temperature

understanding

experiment

explanation

oxygen

_____
bonus word

_____
bonus word

Spelling List

This Week's Focus:
- Spell words with consonant blends
- Spell two-syllable words

STEP 1 Read and Spell	STEP 2 Copy and Spell	STEP 3 Cover and Spell

fold

1. bridge

2. gravity

3. hungry

4. eclipse

5. secret

6. applaud

7. laundry

8. trouble

9. attract

10. twilight

11. between

12. describe

13. snowflake

14. freedom

15. slimy

16. glance

17. burglar

18. switch

19. _____
      bonus word

20. _____
      bonus word

Word Meaning

Fill in the blanks.

bridge	gravity	hungry	eclipse	between
trouble	attract	laundry	twilight	snowflake
freedom	slimy	glance	burglar	switch

1. The _____ lost his _____ when he was sent to jail.

2. Did you see the _____ of the sun?

3. The _____ was pretty to look at before it melted.

4. The boy was so _____ that he ate _____ meals.

5. White flowers _____ moths after _____.

6. She took one _____ at the _____ worm and screamed.

7. I had so many dirty clothes that I had _____ finishing my _____ in time for the party.

My Spelling Dictation

Write the sentences. Circle the spelling words.

1. _____

_____

_____

2. _____

_____

_____

Word Study

Fill in the missing letters to make spelling words.

> br   gr   tr   tw   fr   gl   sw   sn

1. bur__gl__ar
2. _____ance
3. _____ouble
4. _____avity

5. hun_____y
6. _____ilight
7. _____eedom
8. _____idge

9. at_____act
10. be_____een
11. _____owflake
12. _____itch

Circle the words with the sound of **e** as in **we**.
Underline the words that have a silent **e** as in **make**.

glance   freedom   snowflake   between

trouble   secret   eclipse   bridge

Match syllables to make spelling words.
Write the complete words on the lines.

1. hun   cret
2. se   gry
3. laun   ble
4. trou   light
5. twi   dry
6. be   dom
7. snow   flake
8. free   tween

1. _____hungry_____
2. _____
3. _____
4. _____
5. _____
6. _____
7. _____
8. _____

Edit for Spelling

Circle the word in each row that is spelled correctly.

1. freedom — fredom — freedum — ferdom
2. betwen — between — beetwen — betwin
3. twiliht — tylight — twilight — twilite
4. atract — attract — attracte — attrat
5. trouble — truble — troubl — troubel
6. applad — applaude — applawd — applaud
7. bredge — bridg — bridge — brige
8. secrat — secret — seecret — secrit

Circle the misspelled words in the sentences.
Write them correctly on the lines.

1. One glanc at the food and I was hugry.

   _____   _____

2. Would you like to swich to a new lawndry soap?

   _____   _____

3. Please dascribe the slimee bug.

   _____   _____

4. Gravety pulled the snoflak to the ground.

   _____   _____

5. The burgler was caught during an eclips of the sun.

   _____   _____

Building Spelling Skills

Spelling List

This Week's Focus:
- Spell words with consonant digraphs spelled **th**, **ch**, **tch**, and **wh**
- Spell words with the /ər/ sound spelled **er** and **ir**
- Spell words that begin with **spr** and **thr**

STEP 1 Read and Spell	STEP 2 Copy and Spell	STEP 3 Cover and Spell

fold

1. attach
2. where
3. sandwich
4. change
5. watch
6. singer
7. slippery
8. spring
9. gather
10. these
11. thread
12. athlete
13. worth
14. thirsty
15. whisper
16. whistle
17. awhile
18. nowhere
19. _____
    bonus word
20. _____
    bonus word

Word Meaning

Fill in the blanks.

1. Do you know _____ he put the bottle of _____ water?
(where, nowhere)   (spring, these)

2. The _____ wanted to rest _____.
(worth, athlete)   (awhile, nowhere)

3. Blow your _____ and have the students _____ by the flagpole.
(whisper, whistle)   (attach, gather)

4. Would you please _____ _____ children?
(watch, where)   (nowhere, these)

5. I don't like peanut butter. May I _____ my _____?
(attach, change)   (thread, sandwich)

6. The _____ performs the song in a _____.
(worth, singer)   (whisper, nowhere)

7. He was _____, but there was _____ in the desert to get a drink.
(attach, thirsty)   (nowhere, where)

8. The slide isn't _____ much if it isn't _____.
(worth, attach)   (slippery, thread)

My Spelling Dictation

Write the sentences. Circle the spelling words.

1. _____

_____

_____

2. _____

_____

_____

Word Study

Answer the questions using spelling words.

1. Which words contain the digraph **th**?
   Circle every **th** that has the sound you hear in **thin** or **the**.

   _____these_____   _____   _____

   _____   _____   _____

2. Which words contain the digraph **ch**?
   Circle every **ch** that has the sound you hear in **chin**.

   _____   _____   _____

3. Which word contains the digraph **tch**?
   Circle the **tch** that has the sound you hear in **catch**.

   _____

4. Which words contain the digraph **wh**?

   _____   _____   _____

   _____   _____

Fill in the missing digraphs to make spelling words.

th	ch	tch	wh

1. no_____ere

2. _____irsty

3. wa_____

4. _____ere

5. atta_____

6. a_____ile

7. wor_____

8. ga_____er

9. _____ange

10. _____ese

11. _____read

12. _____isper

13. sandwi_____

14. a_____lete

15. _____istle

Edit for Spelling

Underline the words that are spelled correctly.

sandwitch	singor	slippery
worth	awile	thes
spring	wisper	nowhere
wach	whistle	thursty

Circle the misspelled words in the sentences.
Write them correctly on the lines.

1. Atach a note to the sack containing the sandwech.

   _____ _____

2. The athle was thirsdy.

   _____ _____

3. Everyone wached the singr.

   _____ _____

4. Please whispor awile before the play begins.

   _____ _____

5. No where are seashells wurth more than here.

   _____ _____

6. I like to whistel when winter changs to spring.

   _____ _____

Spelling List

This Week's Focus:
- Spell words with the short **a** sound
- Spell words with the long **a** sound spelled **a**, **ai**, **ay**, **eigh**, and **ei**

STEP 1 Read and Spell	STEP 2 Copy and Spell	STEP 3 Cover and Spell
1. fact		
2. began		
3. clasp		
4. rapid		
5. able		
6. later		
7. space		
8. stranger		
9. grade		
10. display		
11. main		
12. explain		
13. freight		
14. neighbor		
15. weigh		
16. vein		
17. April		
18. ankle		
19. _____ bonus word		
20. _____ bonus word		

fold

Word Meaning

Fill in the blanks.

able	space	stranger	grade	display
explain	neighbor	weigh	April	ankle

1. I'm in the fourth _____ at school.

2. My next-door _____ moved in during the month of _____.

3. My mom says to never talk to a _____.

4. Let me _____ why I want to borrow a dollar.

5. I hurt my _____, but I'm _____ to walk on it.

6. I _____ 60 pounds.

7. I will put my dog on _____ at the next dog show.

8. My dentist said I didn't have enough _____ between my teeth.

My Spelling Dictation

Write the sentences. Circle the spelling words.

1. _____

_____

_____

2. _____

_____

_____

Word Study

List the spelling words with the sound of long **a**.
Then circle the letters that make the long **a** sound. Circle the letters **a**, **ai**, **ay**, **ei**, or **eigh**.

1. _____explain_____

2. _____

3. _____

4. _____

5. _____

6. _____

7. _____

8. _____

9. _____

10. _____

11. _____

12. _____

13. _____

List the spelling words with the sound of short **a**. Then circle the letters that make the short **a** sound.

1. _____

2. _____

3. _____

4. _____

5. _____

Match syllables to make words. Write the complete word on the line.

1. neigh	play	1. _____
2. dis	bor	2. _____
3. be	ger	3. _____
4. ex	id	4. _____
5. stran	gan	5. _____
6. rap	plain	6. _____

30

Edit for Spelling

Circle the 15 misspelled words in the story below.
Write them correctly on the lines.

April's Space Report

April wrote a report and made a dicplay about spac. Her report begain with many facs. She explained how much a person would weighe on the moon, the rapide speed of light, and even strangor things. Her display had one mane feature, a picture of the freigt the space shuttle carries.

All of Apirl's hard work was rewarded. Her project was given an A grad. Latter that afternoon, April showed her project to her naighbor. Her nayhbor gave April a big hug.

_____   _____

_____   _____

_____   _____

_____   _____

_____   _____

_____   _____

_____   _____

_____

WEEK 4

Spelling List

This Week's Focus:
- Spell words with the short **e** sound
- Spell words with the long **e** sound spelled **ea**, **ee**, **ei**, **ie**, **e**, and **eo**

STEP 1 Read and Spell

STEP 2 Copy and Spell

STEP 3 Cover and Spell

fold

1. then
2. else
3. edge
4. when
5. tenth
6. empty
7. sketch
8. spelling
9. easy
10. eager
11. sneakers
12. mean
13. fifteen
14. receive
15. piece
16. believe
17. people
18. squeeze
19. _____
   bonus word
20. _____
   bonus word

Word Meaning

Fill in the blanks with spelling words.

else	when	tenth	empty
sketch	easy	eager	sneakers
mean	fifteen	receive	piece
believe	spelling	people	squeeze

1. Fred tried to _____ all the juice out of the _____ of fruit.

2. What _____ could the _____ do but laugh?

3. There were _____ runners in the race. Frederica came in _____.

4. How many _____ words do you _____ you can spell correctly?

5. Does the _____ bag _____ that someone took our lunch?

6. Fred was always _____ to _____ pictures in art class.

7. The athlete found running _____ when she wore _____.

8. _____ will you _____ the letter?

My Spelling Dictation

Write the sentences. Circle the spelling words.

1. _____

   _____

   _____

2. _____

   _____

   _____

Word Study

Underline the words with the long **e** sound.
Circle the letters that make the long **e** sound. Circle the letters **e**, **ee**, **ie**, **ea**, **ei**, **eo**, or **y**.

1. squeeze	6. sneakers	11. mean	16. spelling
2. else	7. sketch	12. fifteen	17. people
3. believe	8. easy	13. receive	18. then
4. when	9. eager	14. piece	
5. tenth	10. empty	15. edge	

Underline the words with the same vowel sound you hear in **bed**.
Circle the letter that makes that sound.

1. when	6. edge	11. else	16. easy
2. mean	7. sketch	12. fifteen	17. people
3. believe	8. spelling	13. eager	18. then
4. piece	9. receive	14. squeeze	
5. empty	10. tenth	15. sneakers	

Write the correct spelling for the long **e** sound in these words. Write **ie** or **ei**.

bel_____ve   rec_____ve   p_____ce

Write the spelling words that mean about the same as these words.

1. grip   _____
2. enthusiastic _____
3. part   _____
4. void   _____
5. get   _____

6. unkind   _____
7. trust   _____
8. drawing   _____
9. border   _____
10. effortless   _____

Edit for Spelling

Circle the word in each row that is spelled correctly.

1. beleive	believ	believe	beleev
2. peice	piece	piec	pece
3. receive	recieve	reciev	resieve
4. eles	else	alse	ellse
5. easy	easee	esy	eazy
6. scetch	skech	skecth	sketch
7. imty	emty	empty	emptey
8. meen	mean	mene	meane
9. squeze	squeez	squeeze	skweez
10. spelling	speling	spellin	speleling
11. peaple	people	peple	peopel
12. eager	eger	eagar	aeger

Circle the misspelled words in the sentences. Write them correctly on the lines.

1. I was the tanth in a line of fifeteen peple.

   _____   _____   _____

2. My sneekers got wet. Than my socks got wet.

   _____   _____

3. Whin did you want to play at my house?

   _____

4. Do you know what els will happen if you stand too close to the edg?

   _____   _____

Building Spelling Skills

Spelling List

This Week's Focus:
- Spell words with the short **i** sound
- Spell words with the long **i** sound spelled **i**, **y**, **igh**, and **uy**

STEP 1 Read and Spell	**STEP 2** Copy and Spell	**STEP 3** Cover and Spell
1. since		
2. which		
3. inch		
4. string		
5. picnic		
6. shrimp		
7. title		
8. mind		
9. wild		
10. decide		
11. why		
12. skyscraper		
13. buy		
14. right		
15. lightning		
16. write		
17. cypress		
18. bicycle		
19. _____ bonus word		
20. _____ bonus word		

fold

Word Meaning

Complete the crossword puzzle using spelling words.

Down

1. to purchase
2. the name of a book
3. _____ one?
5. a thin rope; cord
6. an outdoor meal
9. not tame

Across

3. a question word
4. a measurement
5. a building
7. to make up your mind
8. from then until now
9. to put words on paper
10. correct

My Spelling Dictation

Write the sentences. Circle the spelling words.

1. _____

_____

_____

2. _____

_____

_____

Word Study

Write the spelling words in the correct column.

mind	bicycle	shrimp	title	decide
inch	which	since	wild	cypress
why	skyscraper	buy	string	
picnic	lightning	write	right	

i as in **fix**	**i** as in **pie**
_____	_____
_____	_____
_____	_____
_____	_____
_____	_____
_____	_____
_____	_____
	_____
	_____
	_____
	_____

Match syllables to make words. Write the complete words on the lines.

1. ti   cide   1. _____
2. pic   ning   2. _____
3. de   tle   3. _____
4. light   nic   4. _____
5. cy   press   5. _____

Edit for Spelling

Circle the word in each row that is spelled correctly.

1. sens	cince	since	senc
2. writ	write	rite	rwrit
3. string	streng	strin	streg
4. titl	titel	tittle	title

Circle the 11 misspelled words below.
Write them correctly on the lines.

One Bad Picnic

The picnc was wilde. Wy, you ask? First, my bicyle had a flat on the way there. Second, there was liting and an inc of rain on the ground. Third, I couldn't dicide whitch to eat, shremp or fish. Fourth, a skiscraper blocked the sun. Finally, a cipress tree fell on our table.

_____   _____

_____   _____

_____   _____

_____   _____

_____

Spelling List

This Week's Focus:
- Spell words with the short **o** sound
- Spell words with the long **o** sound spelled **o**, **ow**, **oa**, **ou**, and **oe**

STEP 1 Read and Spell	STEP 2 Copy and Spell	STEP 3 Cover and Spell

fold

1. strong

2. wrong

3. copy

4. cloth

5. problem

6. bottom

7. whole

8. explode

9. control

10. shown

11. bowl

12. October

13. smoky

14. coach

15. throat

16. toast

17. doughnut

18. foe

19. _____
bonus word

20. _____
bonus word

Word Meaning

Answer the questions using spelling words.

1. Which spelling word is the antonym for...?

   a. weak _____

   b. part _____

   c. give freedom _____

   d. do differently _____

   e. solution _____

   f. right _____

   g. top _____

   h. friend _____

2. What do you call...?

   a. a month in the fall _____

   b. an object that holds breakfast cereal _____

   c. a pastry with a hole in it _____

   d. warm, browned bread _____

   e. material for making clothes _____

   f. the part of the body food goes down _____

   g. a person who teaches soccer _____

My Spelling Dictation

Write the sentences. Circle the spelling words.

1. _____

   _____

   _____

2. _____

   _____

   _____

Word Study

Write the spelling words in the correct column.

strong	foe	wrong	doughnut
throat	toast	coach	cloth
problem	copy	smoky	whole
explode	shown	bowl	bottom

o as in **fox**

_____

_____

_____

_____

_____

_____

o as in **hope**

_____

_____

_____

_____

_____

_____

_____

_____

Circle the silent letter or letters in each word.

wrong   whole   shown   bowl

explode   doughnut   foe   throat

Edit for Spelling

Circle the misspelled words in the sentences.
Write them correctly on the lines.

1. I enjoy eating a donat on a cold octobr morning.

   _____   _____

2. What went rong with the strang rope?

   _____   _____

3. Copee that probelm.

   _____   _____

4. I was shoan where to put my boal.

   _____   _____

5. The coch car on the train was too smokey.

   _____   _____

6. Are you a friend or fo?

   _____

7. The tost got stuck in my throt.

   _____   _____

8. The hole battom of my pants got wet.

   _____   _____

9. I watched the fireworks explod.

   _____

Building Spelling Skills

Spelling List

This Week's Focus:
- Spell words with the short **u** sound
- Spell words with the long **u** sound spelled **ue**, **u**, and **eau**

STEP 1 Read and Spell

1. blush
2. crutch
3. crunch
4. grumpy
5. much
6. umpire
7. uncle
8. none
9. does
10. fuel
11. cute
12. cubicle
13. human
14. future
15. usual
16. uniform
17. used
18. beautiful
19. _____ bonus word
20. _____ bonus word

fold

STEP 2 Copy and Spell

STEP 3 Cover and Spell

Word Meaning

Write the letter of the meaning on the line
in front of the spelling word.

_____ 1. blush	a. to grind or chew
_____ 2. crutch	b. irritable
_____ 3. crunch	c. to turn pink
_____ 4. grumpy	d. a parent's brother
_____ 5. much	e. zero
_____ 6. umpire	f. a person
_____ 7. uncle	g. the time ahead
_____ 8. none	h. many in number
_____ 9. does	i. a sports judge
_____ 10. fuel	j. common
_____ 11. cute	k. performs an action
_____ 12. cubicle	l. adorable
_____ 13. human	m. a small space
_____ 14. future	n. a support
_____ 15. usual	o. an energy source

My Spelling Dictation

Write the sentences. Circle the spelling words.

1. _____

   _____

   _____

2. _____

   _____

   _____

Word Study

Write the spelling words in the correct column.

blush	uniform	usual	crutch
crunch	human	grumpy	cubicle
cute	much	fuel	uncle
umpire	none	does	used

u as in cup

_____

_____

_____

_____

_____

_____

_____

_____

u as in use

_____

_____

_____

_____

_____

_____

_____

Match syllables to make spelling words.
Write the complete words on the lines.

1. grum   ture   _____

2. um   man   _____

3. hu   cle   _____

4. un   pire   _____

5. fu   py   _____

6. beau   u   ful   _____

7. un   i   al   _____

8. us   i   cle   _____

9. cub   ti   form   _____

Edit for Spelling

Circle the 12 misspelled words below.
Write them correctly on the lines.

Soccer Is a Wonderful Game

Unless…

Your uncl says your unifurm is cut.

There's no fule in the van so non of the team players show up on time

for the game.

The umpir is grompy.

The beutiful playing field is covered in mud.

You hear a crunh when you kick the ball.

You blash when you slip and fall.

You need a cruth to get off the field.

And finally, you don't get to play mutch.

_____   _____

_____   _____

_____   _____

_____   _____

_____   _____

_____   _____

WEEK 8

Spelling List

This Week's Focus:
- Spell words with double consonants
- Divide words with double consonants into syllables

fold

1. follow

2. matter

3. summer

4. million

5. dollar

6. scissors

7. cattle

8. address

9. office

10. suppertime

11. blizzard

12. penny

13. wrapper

14. wallet

15. occurrence

16. village

17. collide

18. battle

19. _____
   bonus word

20. _____
   bonus word

Word Meaning

Complete the crossword puzzle using spelling words.

Down

1. a place of employment
3. the location of a building
4. to go behind
6. material
8. a large number
10. less than a nickel

Across

2. a small town
5. a happening
7. a season
9. 8 quarters = 2 _____
11. a container for money
12. an outer paper covering

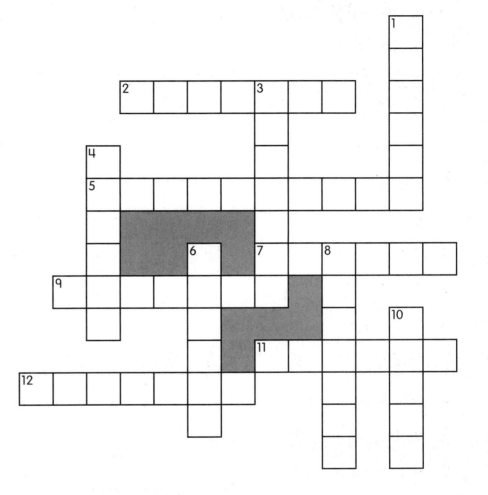

My Spelling Dictation

Write the sentences. Circle the spelling words.

1. _____

_____

_____

2. _____

_____

_____

Word Study

Fill in the missing double letters to make spelling words.

| cc | dd | ff | ll | mm | nn | pp | rr | ss | tt | zz |

1. a_____ress

2. bli_____ard

3. wa_____et

4. co_____ide

5. o_____ice

6. wra_____er

7. pe_____y

8. mi_____ion

9. vi_____age

10. ba_____le

11. fo_____ow

12. sci_____ors

13. ma_____er

14. su_____er

15. ca_____le

16. do_____ar

17. su_____ertime

18. o_____u_____ence

Match syllables to make spelling words.
Write the complete words on the lines.

1. fol   lide   _____

2. bat   low   _____

3. mat   ter   _____

4. col   tle   _____

5. of   tle   _____

6. cat   fice   _____

7. vil   ny   _____

8. wal   lar   _____

9. pen   lage   _____

10. scis   let   _____

11. dol   sors   _____

12. mil   lion   _____

Edit for Spelling

Circle the words that are spelled correctly.

folow	dollar	walet	village
collide	batle	matler	cattle
rapper	peny	occurence	suppertime
million	adress	summer	scisors

Circle the misspelled words in the sentences.
Write them correctly on the lines.

1. My ofice is in a small villag.

   _____   _____

2. My addres is 402 Sumer Lane.

   _____   _____

3. I folow the rule to never run with scisors.

   _____   _____

4. Your change is four dollers and one pennie.

   _____   _____

5. The blizzerd must have had a millon snowflakes.

   _____   _____

6. Did you see the catle batle over that salt lick?

   _____   _____

Building Spelling Skills

WEEK 9

Spelling List

This Week's Focus:
- Spell time and calendar words
- Identify word origins

STEP 1 Read and Spell	STEP 2 Copy and Spell	STEP 3 Cover and Spell

fold

1. Tuesday

2. Wednesday

3. Thursday

4. Saturday

5. January

6. February

7. July

8. August

9. September

10. November

11. month

12. year

13. holiday

14. autumn

15. season

16. calendar

17. second

18. minute

19. _____
    bonus word

20. _____
    bonus word

Word Meaning

Answer these questions using spelling words.

1. Name the months.

   a. _____   d. _____

   b. _____   e. _____

   c. _____   f. _____

2. Name the days of the week.

   a. _____   c. _____

   b. _____   d. _____

3. What has 12 months in it?

   _____

4. What has about 30 days in it?

   _____

Fill in the blanks using spelling words.

1. Autumn is one of the four _____.

2. A _____ can be used to know the day and date.

My Spelling Dictation

Write the sentences. Circle the spelling words.

1. _____

   _____

   _____

2. _____

   _____

   _____

The days of the week are named for the sun, moon, and figures from mythology.
Write the letter of the word origin on the line in front of the day.

_____ 1. Sunday	a. moon
_____ 2. Monday	b. Tiu, god of war
_____ 3. Tuesday	c. sun
_____ 4. Wednesday	d. Saturn, Roman god of farming
_____ 5. Thursday	e. Freya, Norse goddess of love
_____ 6. Friday	f. Thor, Norse god of thunder
_____ 7. Saturday	g. Woden, king of the Norse gods

The names of the months come from Latin, the language spoken in ancient Rome.
Write the letter of the Latin word on the line in front of the month.

_____ 1. January	a. octo
_____ 2. February	b. decem
_____ 3. March	c. februa
_____ 4. April	d. septem
_____ 5. May	e. novem
_____ 6. June	f. Janus
_____ 7. July	g. aprilis
_____ 8. August	h. Maia
_____ 9. September	i. Mars
_____ 10. October	j. Juno
_____ 11. November	k. named after Augustus Caesar
_____ 12. December	l. named after Julius Caesar

54

Edit for Spelling

Circle the words that are spelled correctly.

September	seeson	calendr	holiday
year	month	Thursdey	Tuesday
atumn	Augest	July	Satureday
February	second	minate	Wednesday

Circle the misspelled words in the sentences.
Write them correctly on the lines.

1. Our holeday starts on Wednsday.

   _____   _____

2. Please find the mounth of Janary on the calendar.

   _____   _____

3. How many mintes and seconts did I take to run four laps?

   _____   _____

4. Tusday and Thersday are the days we have art class.

   _____   _____

5. Juli 4th is an important day in the United States.

   _____

6. I enjoy watching Satarday morning cartoons.

   _____

Spelling List

This Week's Focus:
- Spell words with the schwa sound
- Spell words with the short **u** sound spelled **o**

STEP 1 Read and Spell	STEP 2 Copy and Spell	STEP 3 Cover and Spell

fold

1. across
2. alone
3. among
4. brother
5. again
6. front
7. banana
8. appear
9. compass
10. pedal
11. given
12. heaven
13. mountain
14. ocean
15. cousin
16. purchase
17. often
18. color
19. _____ bonus word
20. _____ bonus word

Word Meaning

Fill in the blanks with spelling words.

1. I went to the store to _____ a yellow _____.

2. I use a _____ to navigate my boat on the _____.

3. I had to _____ my bike _____ a bridge.

4. The climber reached the peak of the _____.

5. When my puppy is left _____, he starts to whine.

6. How _____ do you think the puppy will whine tonight?

7. I was _____ a red flower. That is my favorite _____.

8. Do you know my _____ and my _____?

9. Who will _____ when we knock on the _____ door?

10. I hope to see you _____ tomorrow.

My Spelling Dictation

Write the sentences. Circle the spelling words.

1. _____

_____

_____

2. _____

_____

_____

Word Study

Write the symbol ə over the letter or letters that make the schwa sound.

ə

across	alone	among	again
about	appear	brother	banana
compass	heaven	mountain	ocean
cousin	given	often	

Divide these words into syllables.

1. across   a cross

2. alone _____

3. among _____

4. again _____

5. appear _____

6. mountain _____

7. brother _____

8. compass _____

9. banana _____

10. given _____

11. heaven _____

12. ocean _____

13. cousin _____

14. purchase _____

15. often _____

16. color _____

17. pedal _____

Edit for Spelling

Circle the word in each row that is spelled correctly.

1. heven   heaven   heavan   heavun

2. ocean   ocein   osean   oshun

3. collor   colar   coler   color

4. pedel   pedal   pedle   peddel

5. apear   apper   appere   appear

6. again   agin   agan   ugin

7. bananna   banana   banaana   bannana

8. frunt   frant   front   phrunt

Circle the misspelled words in the sentences.
Write them correctly on the lines.

1. My cousan, brothur, and I went on a hike acros the mowntens.

   _____   _____

   _____   _____

2. We pruchased a compas so we wouldn't get lost amung all the trees.

   _____   _____   _____

3. It was awful to be all alon at night in the forest.

   _____

4. How ofton would you go on a hike if you were givan the chance?

   _____   _____

This Week's Focus:
• Spell contractions

STEP 1 Read and Spell

fold

STEP 2 Copy and Spell

STEP 3 Cover and Spell

1. didn't

2. that's

3. they're

4. you're

5. couldn't

6. haven't

7. o'clock

8. we're

9. isn't

10. I'm

11. it's

12. who's

13. they'd

14. could've

15. they've

16. you'll

17. don't

18. aren't

19. _____
   bonus word

20. _____
   bonus word

Word Meaning

Fill in the blanks with spelling words.

1. _____ all done with my homework.

2. I _____ want to do homework after 7 _____.

3. I wonder _____ knocking at the door?

4. Why _____ you playing outside?

5. It _____ my job to clean your room.

6. _____ anyone see what happened?

7. _____ time to go to school.

8. _____ going to our dance class.

9. _____ my best friend.

My Spelling Dictation

Write the sentences. Circle the spelling words.

1. _____

_____

_____

2. _____

_____

_____

A contraction is a word formed from two words by leaving
out some letters. Use an apostrophe to replace any missing letters.

Write the contraction. Then write the missing letter or letters.

1. are not   _____aren't_____   __o__

2. do not   _____   _____

3. you will   _____   _____

4. they have   _____   _____

5. could have   _____   _____

6. they would   _____   _____

7. who is   _____   _____

8. it is   _____   _____

9. I am   _____   _____

10. is not   _____   _____

11. we are   _____   _____

12. of the clock   _____   _____

13. have not   _____   _____

14. could not   _____   _____

15. you are   _____   _____

16. they are   _____   _____

17. that is   _____   _____

18. did not   _____   _____

Edit for Spelling

Write the missing apostrophe in the correct place.

1. Im
2. its
3. whos
4. theyd
5. couldve
6. theyve

7. youll
8. dont
9. arent
10. isnt
11. were
12. oclock

13. havent
14. couldnt
15. youre
16. thats
17. theyre
18. didnt

Circle the misspelled words in the sentences.
Write them correctly on the lines.

1. Please doen't sit in that chair.

_____

2. Thay're going to the store at 4 ol'clock.

_____ _____

3. Who'se seen my cat? I doen't know where he's gone!

_____ _____

4. You'r my best friend. Were' always having fun together.

_____ _____

5. Thats what Im' going to do. You'l want to do it, too. Its fun.

_____ _____

_____ _____

Spelling List

This Week's Focus:
- Spell compound words

STEP 1 Read and Spell	STEP 2 Copy and Spell	STEP 3 Cover and Spell

fold

1. anyone
2. however
3. everything
4. himself
5. birthday
6. herself
7. somewhere
8. afternoon
9. chalkboard
10. daydream
11. downstairs
12. grandparents
13. breakfast
14. outfield
15. scarecrow
16. nobody
17. dragonfly
18. keyboard
19. _____
   bonus word
20. _____
   bonus word

64

Word Meaning

Complete the crossword puzzle using spelling words.

Down

1. in baseball, the area farthest from home plate
2. an early meal
3. a celebration
5. an insect
6. fantasy
7. where fingers go on computers

Across

4. the opposite of **herself**
8. one of your parents' parents
9. no one
10. any person
11. a figure made of straw

My Spelling Dictation

Write the sentences. Circle the spelling words.

1. _____

   _____

   _____

2. _____

   _____

   _____

Word Study

A compound word is made from two shorter words.

Use one word from each column to make compound words. Cross out each word as you use it.
Check your spelling to make sure that you form the compound words correctly.

Column 1	Column 2	Compound Words
chalk	parents	1. _____
some	noon	2. _____
after	ever	3. _____
how	self	4. _____
her	where	5. _____
grand	board	6. _____

Place a / between the parts of these compound words.

1. any/one
2. however
3. everything
4. himself
5. birthday
6. herself
7. somewhere
8. afternoon
9. chalkboard

10. daydream
11. downstairs
12. grandparents
13. breakfast
14. outfield
15. scarecrow
16. nobody
17. dragonfly
18. keyboard

Edit for Spelling

Circle the misspelled words in the sentences.
Write them correctly on the lines.

1. Will any one who is having a birth day please stand up?

   _____   _____

2. She wanted to do it her self. He wanted to do it hemself.

   _____   _____

3. This is every thing a dragon fly would eat.

   _____   _____

4. Somwhere on my key borad is the key I need.

   _____   _____

5. The teacher wrote the word "outfeild" on the chalk board.

   _____   _____

6. No body knew the name of the scarcrow.

   _____   _____

7. My grandparants always have break fast early in the morning.

   _____   _____

8. He was day dreaming down stairs in a soft chair.

   _____   _____

Circle the word in each row that is spelled correctly.

1. out field	outfield	out-field	outfeild
2. afternoon	after noon	after-noon	afternun
3. every-thing	every thing	evrything	everything
4. brakefast	breakfast	break fast	break-fast
5. no body	no-body	nobody	noobody

Building Spelling Skills

WEEK 13

Spelling List

This Week's Focus:
• Spell words with the endings **-ing** and **-ed**

STEP 1 Read and Spell	STEP 2 Copy and Spell	STEP 3 Cover and Spell
1. lived		
2. living		
3. rattled		
4. rattling		
5. studied		
6. studying		
7. traveled		
8. traveling		
9. changed		
10. changing		
11. appeared		
12. appearing		
13. raced		
14. racing		
15. hoped		
16. hoping		
17. wrapped		
18. wrapping		
19. _____ bonus word		
20. _____ bonus word		

fold

Building Spelling Skills, Daily Practice • EMC 2708   68   © Evan-Moor Corp.

Word Meaning

Complete these tasks using spelling words.

1. Write three verbs that are in the present tense.

   _____   _____   _____

2. Write three verbs that are in the past tense.

   _____   _____   _____

3. Write the base word that means...

   a. to go on a journey   _____

   b. to learn   _____

   c. to move quickly   _____

   d. to switch or alter   _____

   e. to exist   _____

   f. to wish   _____

   g. to clatter   _____

   h. to show up   _____

My Spelling Dictation

Write the sentences. Circle the spelling words.

1. _____

   _____

   _____

2. _____

   _____

   _____

Word Study

Add **ing** to the base words. Write the new word on the line.
Check the box that shows how you changed the word.

	no change	drop **e**	double final consonant
1. live living		✔	
2. wrap			
3. rattle			
4. hope			
5. study			
6. race			
7. travel			
8. change			
9. appear			

Add **ed** to the base words. Write the new word on the line.
Check the box that shows how you changed the word.

	no change	change **y** to **i**	drop **e**	double final consonant
1. live				
2. wrap				
3. rattle				
4. hope				
5. study				
6. race				
7. travel				
8. change				
9. appear				

Edit for Spelling

Circle the word in each row that is spelled correctly.

1. rattling   ratling   ratteling   rattlling

2. raceing   racing   rasing   rassing

3. travelled   travvled   travled   traveled

4. chanjing   changeing   changing   changeng

5. apearing   appearing   appearring   appering

Circle the 8 misspelled words below.
Write the words correctly on the lines.

Changing Appearances

Ian was travel down a dirt road. He race to one side of the road and saw a tiny object hanging from a tree branch. He study the object for a long time. After a while, it changd. The wraping around the object split open. Perhaps, Ian thought, something live inside and wanted out. Right before Ian's eyes appear a butterfly. It was beautiful! Ian hope he would see the butterfly again someday.

_____ _____

_____ _____

_____ _____

_____ _____

Spelling List

This Week's Focus:
- Spell words with the endings **-er** and **-est**

STEP 1 Read and Spell	STEP 2 Copy and Spell	STEP 3 Cover and Spell

fold

1. cleaner
2. cleanest
3. bigger
4. biggest
5. earlier
6. earliest
7. quicker
8. quickest
9. busier
10. busiest
11. rougher
12. roughest
13. heavier
14. heaviest
15. happier
16. happiest
17. lazier
18. laziest
19. _____
    bonus word
20. _____
    bonus word

Word Meaning

Complete the crossword puzzle using spelling words.

Down

1. less active than another person
2. doing more than anyone
3. larger than another thing
5. less smooth
7. more spotless
8. arriving before another person

Across

4. larger than anything
6. the opposite of **smoothest**
7. the most spotless
9. arriving before anyone
10. more weighty

My Spelling Dictation

Write the sentences. Circle the spelling words.

1. _____

_____

_____

2. _____

_____

_____

Word Study

Add **er** to the base words. Write the new word on the line.
Check the box that shows how you changed the word.

	no change	change **y** to **i**	double final consonant
1. clean _____			
2. big _____			
3. early _____			
4. quick _____			
5. busy _____			
6. rough _____			
7. heavy _____			
8. happy _____			
9. lazy _____			

Add **est** to the base words. Write the new word on the line.
Check the box that shows how you changed the word.

	no change	change **y** to **i**	double final consonant
1. clean _____			
2. big _____			
3. early _____			
4. quick _____			
5. busy _____			
6. rough _____			
7. heavy _____			
8. happy _____			
9. lazy _____			

Edit for Spelling

Circle the words that are spelled correctly.

earlyest	busy	biggiest	quick
heaviest	besiest	biggier	quicker
lazy	buser	cleanest	happyest
lazyest	roughest	cleanier	happiest

Circle the incorrect word in each sentence.
Write it correctly on the line.

1. My dog is biggest than your dog. _____

2. I'm the earlest person here. _____

3. This is the lazier turtle in the zoo. _____

4. Who is happyer, Angela or Elizabeth? _____

5. My rock is heaviest than your rock. _____

6. I'm busyest in the summer. _____

7. Which way is the quickiest? _____

8. You have the cleaniest room in the house! _____

9. This wood feels roughor than that wood. _____

10. You seem to be the hapiest person here. _____

11. The teacher looks busyer than the students. _____

Building Spelling Skills

WEEK 15

Spelling List

This Week's Focus:
- Spell words with the /ur/ sound spelled **er**, **ir**, **ur**, **ear**, **or**, and **ar**

STEP 1 Read and Spell

1. early
2. earth
3. search
4. service
5. wonder
6. surface
7. curly
8. shirt
9. thirty
10. doctor
11. sailor
12. shower
13. bakery
14. another
15. barber
16. collar
17. worse
18. world
19. _____
   bonus word
20. _____
   bonus word

fold

STEP 2 Copy and Spell

STEP 3 Cover and Spell

Word Meaning

Fill in the blanks with spelling words.

1. Before you wash your _____, rub soap on the _____.

2. There's nothing _____ in this _____ than wobbly skates.

3. The _____ told the _____ he was seasick.

4. The _____ cut off all the boy's _____ hair.

5. The dry _____ welcomes the rain _____.

6. With such bad _____, it is a _____ how this _____ stays in business.

7. The _____ bird usually gets the worm, but this time _____ bird got it.

8. Can a submarine dive _____ miles below the _____ of the ocean?

My Spelling Dictation

Write the sentences. Circle the spelling words.

1. _____

_____

_____

2. _____

_____

_____

Word Study

Fill in the missing letters to make spelling words.

> or   er   ar   ur   ir

1. doct_____

2. barb_____

3. show_____

4. wond_____

5. sail_____

6. anoth_____

7. doll_____

8. s_____vice

9. w_____se

10. bak_____y

11. w_____ld

12. th_____ty

13. c_____ly

14. sh_____t

Divide these words into syllables. Check your answers in a dictionary.

1. early _____ _____

2. thirty _____ _____

3. doctor _____ _____

4. service _____ _____

5. wonder _____ _____

6. barber _____ _____

7. surface _____ _____

8. curly _____ _____

9. sailor _____ _____

10. shower _____ _____

11. dollar _____ _____

12. collar _____ _____

Edit for Spelling

Circle the 12 misspelled words below.
Write them correctly on the lines.

Earth Day Excitement

Ms. Spring brought her class of therty students to an Erth Day workshop. They learned many things about caring for our wurld.

1. A rain showor can wash away the top serface of soil that doesn't have plants growing in it.

2. The survice of a tree docter may be needed to save a sick tree.

3. There's nothing much wors you can do than pollute groundwater.

Ms. Spring's class stayed at the workshop until erly evening. When it was time to go, everyone had to sarch for a missing student. It didn't take long to find her because her bright white sailer suit and cerly red hair stood out in the crowd.

_____   _____

_____   _____

_____   _____

_____   _____

_____   _____

Spelling List

This Week's Focus:
- Spell singular and plural forms of words

STEP 1 Read and Spell	STEP 2 Copy and Spell	STEP 3 Cover and Spell

fold

1. leaf
2. leaves
3. wolf
4. wolves
5. potato
6. potatoes
7. roof
8. roofs
9. family
10. families
11. library
12. libraries
13. journey
14. journeys
15. hero
16. heroes
17. ditch
18. ditches
19. _____
   bonus word
20. _____
   bonus word

Word Meaning

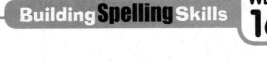

Complete the crossword puzzle using spelling words.

Down
1. several trips
2. a single plant part
3. an admired person
6. parts of plants
7. more than one trench
8. a trench
9. many house coverings
12. a root vegetable

Across
4. several wild canines
5. a single trip
10. several groups of relatives
11. a wild canine
13. persons of great courage
14. more than two root vegetables
15. a house covering

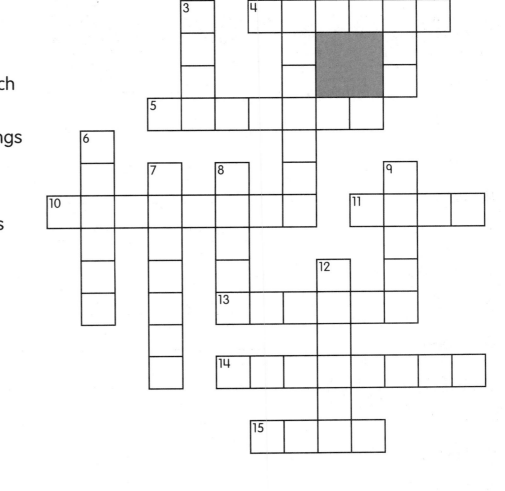

My Spelling Dictation

Write the sentences. Circle the spelling words.

1. _____

_____

_____

2. _____

_____

_____

Word Study

Change each singular noun to its plural form.
Check the box that shows how you changed the word.

	add **s** or **es**	change **y** to **i** add **es**	change **f** to **v** add **es**
1. leaf _____			
2. hero _____			
3. potato _____			
4. family _____			
5. ditch _____			
6. wolf _____			
7. library _____			
8. journey _____			

Divide these words into syllables.

1. heroes _____ _____

2. ditches _____ _____

3. journeys _____ _____

4. potatoes _____ _____ _____

5. families _____ _____ _____

6. libraries _____ _____ _____

Edit for Spelling

Circle the words that are spelled correctly.

familes	libraries	leafs
heros	potatoes	ditches
journeyes	roofes	wolves

Circle the misspelled words in the sentences.
Write them correctly on the lines.

1. My famile looks for aluminum cans in ditchs.

_____   _____

2. The herow of the story ate potatos.

_____   _____

3. There were a lot of leafs on the rooves.

_____   _____

4. The wolfs went on a long journy.

_____   _____

5. All the familes in my neighborhood like to go to the librare.

_____   _____

6. He made one last effort to keep the rouf from catching fire.

_____

7. My dog, who is part woolf, is over there chasing a leef.

_____   _____

8. Books about heros can be found in all libraryes.

_____   _____

Spelling List

This Week's Focus:
• Spell words with the /aw/ sound spelled **al**, **ough**, **o**, **au**, and **aw**

STEP 1 Read and Spell	STEP 2 Copy and Spell	STEP 3 Cover and Spell

fold

1. also
2. bought
3. cough
4. almost
5. false
6. officer
7. soft
8. stalk
9. halt
10. faucet
11. saucer
12. caution
13. lawyer
14. awesome
15. stall
16. crawl
17. awful
18. because
19. _____
   bonus word
20. _____
   bonus word

Word Meaning

Answer the questions using spelling words.

1. Which spelling word is a synonym for…?

    a. too   _____

    b. creep   _____

    c. untrue   _____

    d. gentle   _____

2. Which spelling word is an antonym for…?

    a. hard   _____

    b. go   _____

    c. true   _____

    d. sold   _____

3. Which spelling word means…?

    a. a person who enforces the law

    _____

    b. a plumbing fixture

    _____

    c. a cup's partner

    _____

    d. a person who studies the law

    _____

    e. to expel air noisily

    _____

    f. for the reason that

    _____

    g. in addition

    _____

    h. to move on all fours

    _____

My Spelling Dictation

Write the sentences. Circle the spelling words.

1. _____

   _____

   _____

2. _____

   _____

   _____

Word Study

Write the spelling words in the correct boxes.

also	bought	cough	almost	false	officer
soft	stalk	halt	faucet	saucer	caution
lawyer	awesome	stall	crawl	awful	because

a as in **fall**	**au** as in **caught**	**aw** as in **law**	**o** as in **loft**	**ou** as in **trough**

Match syllables to make words.
Write the complete words on the lines.

1. be   some   1. _____

2. awe   cause   2. _____

3. al   cet   3. _____

4. law   so   4. _____

5. fau   yer   5. _____

6. sau   tion   6. _____

7. cau   most   7. _____

8. al   cer   8. _____

Edit for Spelling

Circle the words that are spelled correctly.

cation	almost	cough	allso
lawyer	oficer	faucet	stalk
fallse	bought	stall	crall
awful	becaus	awesome	saucer

Circle the misspelled words in the sentences.
Write them correctly on the lines.

1. She all most dropped the sawcer.

   _____   _____

2. The layer took great cawtion with the case.

   _____   _____

3. It was awsome to see the baby crall.

   _____   _____

4. He baht a saft blanket.

   _____   _____

5. It was auful to hear him cauf.

   _____   _____

6. The kitchen faucat was dripping becauze it was old.

   _____   _____

7. The offisor yelled, "Hallt!"

   _____   _____

8. That's allso a fallse statement.

   _____   _____

Spelling List

This Week's Focus:
- Spell words with the variant sounds of **c** and **g**

STEP 1 Read and Spell	STEP 2 Copy and Spell	STEP 3 Cover and Spell

fold

1. cinder
2. circle
3. cardinal
4. cereal
5. cycle
6. concert
7. dancer
8. celebrate
9. twice
10. dangerous
11. strange
12. ledge
13. damage
14. geography
15. gentle
16. signal
17. regular
18. sugar
19. _____
   bonus word
20. _____
   bonus word

Word Meaning

Fill in the blanks in the paragraphs below with spelling words.

The Day the Dancer Fell

I have been a _____ for many years. A _____

and _____ situation happened to me one night while I

was performing. I was dancing in a large _____ when a

_____ flew past my head. I was frightened, and stepped too

close to the edge of the stage. I fell into the orchestra pit. Luckily, I had a

_____ landing. I fell right on a gigantic bass drum! There was

no _____ to me or the drum.

Getting Ready to Sing

Every morning I eat a bowl of _____ with two spoonfuls

of _____. I try to put more on, but my dad always gives a

_____ to stop. After breakfast my _____ routine is

to get dressed for school. This morning, however, I must put on my best dress.

I want to look nice when I sing in our school choir _____.

My Spelling Dictation

Write the sentences. Circle the spelling words.

1. _____

_____

_____

2. _____

_____

_____

Word Study

Write the spelling words in the correct boxes.

soft **c** sound as in **face**	hard **c** sound as in **cat**	soft **g** sound as in **giant**	hard **g** sound as in **great**

Write the spelling words that mean about the same as these words.

1. a repeating event _____

2. round _____

3. to honor _____

4. study of the earth _____

5. gesture _____

6. calm _____

7. odd _____

8. harmful _____

Write the spelling words that mean the opposite of these words.

1. repair _____

2. safe _____

3. usual _____

4. harsh _____

Edit for Spelling

Circle the words that are spelled correctly.

strange	sereal	consert
cinder	ledge	sugar
gentel	twise	cycle
cardinal	danser	geographe
regular	damege	dangerous

Circle the misspelled words in the sentences.
Write them correctly on the lines.

1. The dansir leapt twise.

   _____   _____

2. The cardinel ate cerial from my bowl.

   _____   _____

3. It is dangerus to sit on the lege.

   _____   _____

4. The geograpy of the desert was strang.

   _____   _____

5. We used reguler sinder blocks to make the house.

   _____   _____

6. There was a lot of damege to the signel light.

   _____   _____

Spelling List

This Week's Focus:
- Spell words with the /oo/ sound spelled **ew**, **o**, **oe**, **oo**, **ou**, **ough**, **u**, **ue**, and **ui**

STEP 1 Read and Spell	STEP 2 Copy and Spell	STEP 3 Cover and Spell
1. shoes		
2. clues		
3. wound		
4. junior		
5. truth		
6. duty		
7. news		
8. through		
9. few		
10. who		
11. schoolroom		
12. whose		
13. conclusion		
14. June		
15. shampoo		
16. cruel		
17. choose		
18. ruin		
19. _____ bonus word		
20. _____ bonus word		

fold

Word Meaning

Complete the crossword puzzle using spelling words.

Down

1. hints
2. the opposite of **many**
5. to destroy
7. word used when asking about ownership
8. a month
9. to select
11. to hurt

Across

3. responsibility
4. mean
6. information
9. an ending
10. footwear
11. which person?
12. a place to learn

My Spelling Dictation

Write the sentences. Circle the spelling words.

1. _____

_____

_____

2. _____

_____

_____

Word Study

Fill in the missing letters to make spelling words.

ew	o	oe	oo	ou	ough	u	ue	ui

1. f_____

2. sch_____lroom

3. J_____ne

4. cr_____l

5. sh_____s

6. tr_____th

7. d_____ty

8. wh_____

9. ch_____se

10. r_____in

11. thr_____

12. n_____s

13. wh_____se

14. concl_____sion

15. shamp_____

16. w_____nd

17. cl_____s

18. j_____nior

Read each word. Write the number of syllables on the line.

1. shoes _____

2. clues _____

3. wound _____

4. junior _____

5. truth _____

6. duty _____

7. news _____

8. through _____

9. few _____

10. who _____

11. schoolroom _____

12. whose _____

13. conclusion _____

14. June _____

15. shampoo _____

16. cruel _____

17. choose _____

18. ruin _____

Edit for Spelling

Circle the 14 misspelled words below.
Write the words correctly on the lines.

The Big Bell Caper

Mr. Dell's bell was missing from his schoolrom. He used the bell during recess dooty. He would ring his bell to let students know when to return to class. Nuws of the missing bell traveled quickly thrugh the school.

There were feu cloos. Mr. Dell came to the conclosion that he would never see his bell again. The troth was, he was woonded. Whu would be so crul as to take his bell? His students said they would become juinor detectives and help him find his bell before june.

Then a familiar ringing was heard. Ms. Nell, whos room is next door, must have forgotten to tell Mr. Dell that she borrowed his swell bell.

_____   _____

_____   _____

_____   _____

_____   _____

_____   _____

_____   _____

_____   _____

Spelling List

This Week's Focus:
- Spell words with the /oi/ sound spelled **oi** and **oy**
- Spell words with the /ow/ sound spelled **ow** and **ou**

STEP 1 Read and Spell	STEP 2 Copy and Spell	STEP 3 Cover and Spell

fold

1. voice
2. oyster
3. voyage
4. annoy
5. choice
6. avoid
7. appoint
8. enjoy
9. moisture
10. noise
11. drown
12. amount
13. fountain
14. crowded
15. southwest
16. thousand
17. flour
18. pronounce
19. _____
   bonus word
20. _____
   bonus word

Word Meaning

Fill in the blanks with spelling words.

The Meeting

I went to our student council meeting. The room was so _____,

few students had a place to sit. No one could hear what was going on.

The president's _____ was too quiet, and there was lots of

_____ in the room. She had to _____ a sergeant-at-arms

to bring order to the meeting. This helped a lot. Everyone quieted down in

a short _____ of time. After that, the meeting was successful.

The Voyage

Kawa went on an ocean _____ a _____ miles

long. Most of the trip was in the _____ern part of the Pacific Ocean.

And try as she might, she could never learn to _____ the ship's name.

While on the trip, she ate an _____. She especially liked it dipped in

_____ and fried. If she were given the _____, she would

eat them all day long. She will _____ memories of her trip forever.

My Spelling Dictation

Write the sentences. Circle the spelling words.

1. _____

   _____

   _____

2. _____

   _____

   _____

Circle the letters that make the vowel sound in **boy**.

1. v(oi)ce
2. oyster
3. voyage
4. annoy
5. choice

6. avoid
7. appoint
8. enjoy
9. moisture
10. noise

Circle the letters that make the vowel sound in **cow**.

1. drown
2. amount
3. fountain
4. crowded

5. southwest
6. thousand
7. flour
8. pronounce

Match syllables to make spelling words.
Write the complete words on the lines.

1. oys	nounce	1. _____
2. an	ter	2. _____
3. pro	tain	3. _____
4. foun	noy	4. _____
5. a	mount	5. _____
6. thou	ture	6. _____
7. south	sand	7. _____
8. mois	west	8. _____
9. en	age	9. _____
10. voy	joy	10. _____

Edit for Spelling

Circle the word in each row that is spelled correctly.

1. amownt   amount   amunt   umont

2. thousand   thousant   thowsand   thosand

3. injoy   enjoe   enjoi   enjoy

4. voeage   voyage   vowage   voiage

5. voic   voece   voise   voice

6. apoint   appont   appoint   apont

7. pronounce   pronownce   prononce   pronunce

8. sowthwest   southwest   sothwest   south west

Circle the misspelled words in the sentences.
Write them correctly on the lines.

1. Please don't anoy the cat with noice.

    _____   _____

2. Try to avoed putting too much water on the plant. It will droun.

    _____   _____

3. My choece is to eat the oister.

    _____   _____

4. The bag of flowr spilled all over the floor.

    _____

5. The elevator was too crouded.

    _____

6. The weather was so humid that moistur dripped from my glass.

    _____

Spelling List

This Week's Focus:
- Spell words with the /**f**/ sound spelled **f**, **ff**, **ph**, and **gh**

STEP 1 Read and Spell	STEP 2 Copy and Spell	STEP 3 Cover and Spell
1. enough		
2. tougher		
3. fifty		
4. pharmacy		
5. alphabet		
6. nephew		
7. trophy		
8. paragraph		
9. telephone		
10. photograph		
11. giraffe		
12. forest		
13. figure		
14. refrigerator		
15. draft		
16. phrase		
17. traffic		
18. chief		
19. _____ bonus word		
20. _____ bonus word		

fold

Word Meaning

Complete the crossword puzzle using spelling words.

Across

1. a group of words
2. a sufficient amount
4. a leader
7. a section of a piece of writing
10. a drugstore
11. a communication device

Down

1. a picture
3. a relative
5. the number after forty, by tens
6. an award
8. 26 letters
9. a first writing effort

My Spelling Dictation

Write the sentences. Circle the spelling words.

1. _____

_____

_____

2. _____

_____

_____

Word Study

Circle the letters that make the /**f**/ sound.

1. enou(gh)
2. tougher
3. fifty
4. pharmacy
5. alphabet
6. nephew
7. trophy
8. paragraph
9. telephone
10. photograph
11. giraffe
12. forest
13. figure
14. refrigerator
15. draft
16. phrase
17. traffic
18. chief

Fill in the missing letters. Write **f**, **ff**, **gh**, or **ph**.

1. ____f____igure
2. gira____e
3. ____i____ty
4. tra____ic
5. dra____t
6. al____abet
7. paragra____
8. tro____y
9. chie____
10. ____rase
11. re____rigerator
12. ____armacy
13. enou____
14. ____orest
15. ____otogra____
16. tele____one
17. ne____ew
18. tou____er

Edit for Spelling

Circle the 12 misspelled words below.
Write the words correctly on the lines.

The Fifty-Float Chief

The race was on at the soda fountain in Phil's Farmacy. My nehew was trying to make fity root beer floats in less than 15 minutes. The task was toufer than he thought. He figured he had just enouf time to make the final few floats.

There was a fourest of glasses on the counter. People had to stretch their necks like girafes to see the final scoop of ice cream plop into the glass. The splash in the glass was heard just before the buzzer sounded.

My nefew was presented a terrific trophe. The next morning's newspaper had a photograf and a well-written pargraph about his feat. He was named the cheif of root beer floats!

_____   _____

_____   _____

_____   _____

_____   _____

Spelling List

This Week's Focus:
• Spell words with **ight**, **ought**, **aught**, and **au**

STEP 1 Read and Spell	STEP 2 Copy and Spell	STEP 3 Cover and Spell

fold

1. frighten

2. flight

3. brighter

4. flashlight

5. mighty

6. delight

7. tighten

8. nightly

9. sight

10. brought

11. ought

12. thought

13. fought

14. caught

15. daughter

16. taught

17. naughty

18. fault

19. _____
   bonus word

20. _____
   bonus word

Word Meaning

Fill in the blanks with spelling words.
Two of the spelling words are used twice in the story.

The Nightly Fright

A few nights ago, my young _____ _____

she heard a noise coming from our basement. The same thing happened

the next evening. She _____ me to the basement door more

than once, but I never heard a thing. This _____ event,

however, continued to _____ her. One night I decided to

go down the _____ of stairs to see for myself. I shined my

_____ from one corner of the basement to another. Finally,

my light _____ _____ of a pair of yellowish

dots that became _____ and _____. To my

_____, it was just our _____ kitty playing

in a box of yarn. Now my _____ always makes sure the

basement door is closed.

My Spelling Dictation

Write the sentences. Circle the spelling words.

1. _____

   _____

   _____

2. _____

   _____

   _____

Word Study

Add the correct letters to make words.

| ight | ought | aught |

1. fl_____

2. del_____

3. th_____

4. c_____

5. br_____

6. br_____

Circle the letters that make the sound of **a** in **father**.

1. brought

2. fault

3. thought

4. fought

5. caught

6. daughter

7. taught

8. naughty

Circle the letters that make the sound of **i** in **pie**.

1. frighten

2. flight

3. brighter

4. flashlight

5. mighty

6. delight

7. tighten

8. nightly

All the spelling words except one have a pair of silent letters.
What are those letters?

_____ _____

Edit for Spelling

Circle the words that are spelled correctly.

caught	dauhter	thaught	delight
brightor	taught	faught	ought
sight	brihter	frightan	tought

Circle the misspelled words in the sentences.
Write them correctly on the lines.

1. I aught to tighton the lid.

_____ _____

2. It was my fallt that we fouht.

_____ _____

3. I cought a flit to Denver.

_____ _____

4. My daughtor taght her dog to sit up.

_____ _____

5. He used the flashlite nitly.

_____ _____

6. That sieght would frihten anyone.

_____ _____

7. I thougt that child was very naghty.

_____ _____

8. His funny joke broght deliht to the crowd.

_____ _____

9. That toothpaste helped me have a brihter smile.

_____

Spelling List

This Week's Focus:
- Spell words with silent letters

STEP 1 Read and Spell

fold

1. calf
2. walked
3. ghost
4. gnawed
5. climber
6. wreath
7. listen
8. island
9. scent
10. wrench
11. judge
12. fasten
13. wrist
14. doubt
15. knock
16. answer
17. knelt
18. sign
19. _____
    bonus word
20. _____
    bonus word

STEP 2 Copy and Spell

STEP 3 Cover and Spell

Word Meaning

Complete the crossword puzzle using spelling words.
There are three words that are <u>not</u> on your spelling list. Try to figure them out.

Down

1. went onto your knees
2. to secure
3. the reply to a question
4. a circular decoration
5. a baby cow
6. land with water all around it
10. a person who goes up a mountain
11. an object used to unlock a door
12. a body part below the mouth
14. someone who decides cases

Across

4. a tool
7. a smell
8. to hear
9. to taste food
11. to tap on a door
13. strolled
15. a symbol
16. to be unsure
17. the joint above the hand

My Spelling Dictation

Write the sentences. Circle the spelling words.

1. _____

_____

_____

2. _____

_____

_____

Word Study

Circle the letters that are silent.

1. calf
2. walked
3. ghost
4. gnawed
5. climber
6. wreath
7. listen
8. island
9. scent
10. wrench
11. judge
12. fasten
13. wrist
14. doubt
15. knock
16. answer
17. knelt
18. sign

Fill in the missing letters to make spelling words.

> d   b   c   g   k   l   t   w

1. _____nelt
2. _____nock
3. _____rist
4. _____rench
5. _____reath
6. _____nawed
7. si_____n
8. ca_____f
9. wa_____ked
10. clim_____er
11. lis_____en
12. fas_____en
13. ans_____er
14. dou_____t
15. ju_____ge
16. s_____ent

Write the spelling words that mean about the same as these words.

1. strolled _____
2. close _____
3. spirit _____
4. chewed _____
5. hear _____
6. reply _____

Edit for Spelling

Correct the spelling of these words.

1. wrinch _____

2. wreeth _____

3. walkt _____

4. gnawd _____

5. knok _____

6. answor _____

7. dowt _____

8. wrest _____

9. judg _____

10. climbor _____

Circle the misspelled words in the sentences. Write them correctly on the lines.

1. Lisson! Was that a nock at the door?

   _____   _____

2. The caf nelt down to get a drink of water.

   _____   _____

3. I dout that we need a stop sing here.

   _____   _____

4. Did the juge give you an anser?

   _____   _____

5. Did the climer fason the rope correctly?

   _____   _____

6. The iland had the pleasant cent of flowers.

   _____   _____

7. He looked at the watch on his wist before he waked to the store.

   _____   _____

8. She needed to use a rench to put up the large reath.

   _____   _____

Building Spelling Skills

WEEK 24

Spelling List

This Week's Focus:
- Add the suffixes **-ion**, **-tion**, **-sion**, and **-cian** to base words and word roots

STEP 1 Read and Spell

STEP 2 Copy and Spell

STEP 3 Cover and Spell

fold

1. action
2. fiction
3. mission
4. divide
5. division
6. attend
7. attention
8. pollute
9. pollution
10. express
11. expression
12. educate
13. education
14. music
15. musician
16. magic
17. magician
18. physician
19. _____ bonus word
20. _____ bonus word

Word Meaning

Use spelling words to answer the clues.

1. a person who takes care of our physical health _____

2. a person who performs magic _____

3. a person who creates music _____

4. to learn something you must give it this _____

5. teachers want their students to get this _____

6. environmentalists worry about this _____

7. an operation with numbers _____

8. stories that are made up by the author _____

9. an exciting story has lots of this _____

10. something you should use when you read aloud _____

Which spelling word is an antonym for...?

1. clean _____   3. fact _____

2. multiply _____   4. inaction _____

My Spelling Dictation

Write the sentences. Circle the spelling words.

1. _____

_____

_____

2. _____

_____

_____

Word Study

Add the correct suffix to the base word.
You may need to make a change to the base word before adding the suffix.

| ion   tion   sion |

1. An _____ I like is, "It's raining cats and dogs."
   <u>express</u>

2. There is a lot of _____ on the football field.
   <u>act</u>

3. I need your _____.
   <u>attend</u>

4. I enjoy learning about _____ in math class.
   <u>divide</u>

5. My _____ is very important to me.
   <u>educate</u>

6. There is _____ in the river.
   <u>pollute</u>

Write each word from the spelling list in the correct box.

two-syllable words	three-syllable words	four-syllable words

Edit for Spelling

Circle the 20 misspelled words below. Three words are misspelled more than once. Write the words correctly on the lines.

On a Mission

A musicion, a magicion, and a physicion went on a hike in the mountains. The musican said the mountains brought musik to her heart. The magician's expresion was that the mountains were magical. The phsician, however, said the mountains reminded her of sprained ankles.

The muician liked to focus her atention on listening to the songs of the birds. The magikian would always xpres her amazement at how fast chipmunks could disappear. The fasician, however, looked for twigs that could be used for splints.

The musician enjoyed being in a place where there was no sound polution. The magecian enjoyed watching beavers divid tree branches in half. The phasician, however, worried about whether she brought enough poison ivy lotion.

Toward the end of the hike, it became the mision of the musecian and mugician to help the physcian "doctor" her attitude so she could enjoy the remainder of the day.

_____   _____

_____   _____

_____   _____

_____   _____

_____   _____

_____   _____

_____   _____

_____   _____

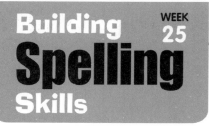

Spelling List

This Week's Focus:
- Spell two- and three-syllable words
- Identify open syllables

STEP 1 Read and Spell

1. lazy
2. volcano
3. flavor
4. piano
5. recent
6. really
7. item
8. pilot
9. triangle
10. climate
11. gigantic
12. program
13. obey
14. puny
15. prepare
16. vacant
17. pulley
18. menu
19. _____
    bonus word
20. _____
    bonus word

fold

STEP 2 Copy and Spell

STEP 3 Cover and Spell

Word Meaning

Fill in the blanks with spelling words.

1. The _____ flew his plane close to the erupting _____.

2. The _____ was so hot and humid that everyone felt _____ and didn't want to work.

3. He played an amazing song on the _____ during the _____.

4. My favorite _____ of ice cream on the _____ is strawberry.

5. They needed a _____ _____ to lift the car.

6. I must _____ dinner for the guests.

7. A _____ study said that juice is _____ good for you.

8. The _____ little dog would always _____ his master.

9. No one lives in the _____ building shaped like a _____.

My Spelling Dictation

Write the sentences. Circle the spelling words.

1. _____

_____

_____

2. _____

_____

_____

Word Study

An open syllable ends with a long vowel sound.
Underline the words that have an open syllable.
Circle the open syllable in each word you underline.

1. la zy
2. volcano
3. flavor
4. piano
5. recent
6. really

7. item
8. pilot
9. triangle
10. climate
11. gigantic
12. program

13. obey
14. puny
15. prepare
16. vacant
17. pulley
18. menu

Fill in the missing letters to make spelling words.

la_____   _____tem   re_____lly   _____gantic

fla_____   _____bey   pi_____o   tri_____gle

Match a first and second syllable to create spelling words.
Write them on the lines.

First	
la	cli
re	o
men	i

Second	
tem	bey
zy	mate
u	cent

_____   _____

_____   _____

_____   _____

Edit for Spelling

Circle the words that are spelled correctly.

climate	giganic	triangal	peano
recent	itum	pilot	puny
vakent	obey	program	realy
laze	volcano	flaver	pully

Circle the misspelled words in the sentences. Write them correctly on the lines.

1. The lawyer was so lasy that he had a vakint office.

   _____   _____

2. Did you see the itam in the newspaper about the valcano?

   _____   _____

3. Which is your favorite flaver, Gigantac Grape or Large Lime?

   _____   _____

4. The pielot realle wants his own plane.

   _____   _____

5. We are pleased with our resent pieno purchase.

   _____   _____

6. Please oby the rules when using that puley.

   _____   _____

7. There's not much on that punee menue.

   _____   _____

8. The climat in the Bermuda Triangel was warm.

   _____   _____

9. He will pripar snacks before watching the TV programe.

   _____   _____

Spelling List

This Week's Focus:
- Spell homophones

STEP 1 Read and Spell	STEP 2 Copy and Spell	STEP 3 Cover and Spell

fold

1. herd
2. heard
3. clothes
4. close
5. hour
6. our
7. two
8. too
9. their
10. there
11. ceiling
12. sealing
13. shoot
14. chute
15. strait
16. straight
17. medal
18. meddle
19. _____ bonus word
20. _____ bonus word

Word Meaning

Complete the crossword puzzle using spelling words.

Down

1. also
3. belonging to them
4. a steep slide; a tight space
5. closing tightly
7. an award
8. listened
9. the opposite of **open**
11. belonging to us
12. the number after **one**

Across

2. a sprout
5. the opposite of **curved**
6. a narrow strip of water
8. a group of cows
9. the top of a room
10. 60 minutes
12. in that place

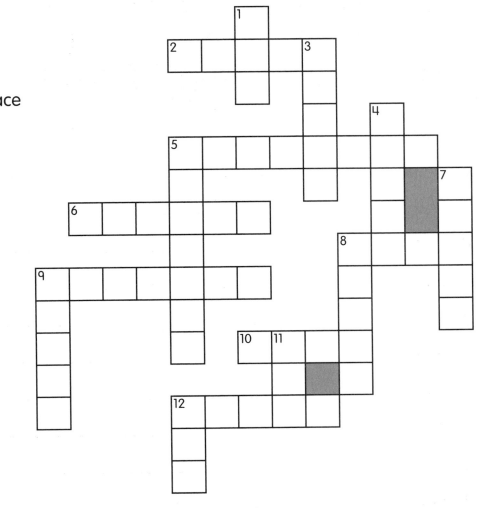

My Spelling Dictation

Write the sentences. Circle the spelling words.

1. _____

    _____

    _____

2. _____

    _____

    _____

Write the spelling words that are homophones for these words.

1. heard _____   4. medal _____   7. sealing _____

2. clothes _____   5. strait _____   8. two _____

3. hour _____   6. chute _____   9. their _____

Choose the correct words to fill in the blanks.

1. I want to go over _____. That box contains _____ toys.
   (their, there)   (their, there)

2. Please be back in one _____. This is _____ house.
   (hour, our)   (hour, our)

3. Let's _____ some hoops. Is the bull in its _____?
   (chute, shoot)   (chute, shoot)

4. I have _____ dogs. She has a dog, _____.
   (two, too)   (two, too)

5. Our boat is in the _____. We're moving _____ ahead.
   (strait, straight)   (strait, straight)

6. Please don't _____ in my problems. He won a _____.
   (meddle, medal)   (meddle, medal)

7. Did you paint the _____? Are you _____ the paint can?
   (sealing, ceiling)   (sealing, ceiling)

8. Do you like _____ clock? One _____ has passed already.
   (our, hour)   (our, hour)

9. Please _____ the closet door. Then put on your _____.
   (close, clothes)   (close, clothes)

Edit for Spelling

Circle the 14 misspelled words below.
Write the words correctly on the lines.

The Dangerous Marble

I'm the marble champion of owr school. Their is no one better. I became a champion because I practice for an our every day. I can shot all the marbles out of a circle in less than too minutes.

During one game, a single "cat's-eye" was left in the circle. My shooter headed straht for it. The impact was so loud that everyone herd it. The marble bounced off the seiling and came way two clos to hitting a group of students who were watching. They ran out of the room like a heard of scared cattle. If they had stayed, they would have been cealing there fate of getting hit by one of my marbles. Sadly, no one saw me receive my medel for winning the game.

_____   _____

_____   _____

_____   _____

_____   _____

_____   _____

_____   _____

Building Spelling Skills

WEEK 27

Spelling List

This Week's Focus:
- Spell words with easily confused spellings

STEP 1 Read and Spell	STEP 2 Copy and Spell	STEP 3 Cover and Spell

fold

1. quiet
2. quite
3. angel
4. angle
5. already
6. all ready
7. desert
8. dessert
9. weather
10. whether
11. pitcher
12. picture
13. loose
14. lose
15. aisle
16. isle
17. dairy
18. diary
19. _____
   bonus word
20. _____
   bonus word

Word Meaning

Choose the correct words to fill in the blanks.

1. Please be _____. You are being _____ noisy.
   (quite, quiet)   (quite, quiet)

2. That's an _____ food cake. Did you measure the _____?
   (angle, angel)   (angle, angel)

3. I've _____ been there. We are _____ to go.
   (all ready, already)   (all ready, already)

4. I love to eat _____. Let's visit the _____.
   (dessert, desert)   (dessert, desert)

5. We're discussing _____ the _____ will clear up.
   (whether, weather)   (whether, weather)

6. Please pass the _____ of water. My _____ is in my wallet.
   (picture, pitcher)   (picture, pitcher)

7. The dog was _____. I don't want to _____ my dog.
   (loose, lose)   (loose, lose)

8. I walked down the _____. I was on a desert _____.
   (isle, aisle)   (isle, aisle)

9. I always take my _____ with me. I work in a _____.
   (diary, dairy)   (diary, dairy)

My Spelling Dictation

Write the sentences. Circle the spelling words.

1. _____

_____

_____

2. _____

_____

_____

Word Study

Circle the word that matches the definition.

1. not noisy   quiet   quite

2. a sharp corner   angel   angle

3. by that time   already   all ready

4. a very dry place   desert   dessert

5. what it's like outside   weather   whether

6. a photograph or drawing   pitcher   picture

7. not tight   loose   lose

8. open space between shelves   aisle   isle

9. a book you write in   dairy   diary

Match syllables to make spelling words.
Write the complete words on the lines.

1. al   gel   1. _____

2. pit   cher   2. _____

3. des   er   3. _____

4. an   ready   4. _____

5. wheth   ert   5. _____

6. weath   er   6. _____

7. qui   sert   7. _____

8. an   et   8. _____

9. des   gle   9. _____

Edit for Spelling

Circle the words that are spelled correctly.

dairy	quiat	angle	wheather
quite	angal	desurt	picture
already	whether	lose	dessert
aile	picher	loose	isle

Circle the misspelled words in the sentences. Write them correctly on the lines.

1. The usher was dancing in the aile.

   _____

2. We listened to the wheather report to know weather we should travel.

   _____   _____

3. The pitchor was in the pictur.

   _____   _____

4. The daire farmer was all readi to milk his herd.

   _____   _____

5. I like to have it quit when I write in my diarry.

   _____   _____

6. We measured that angal alredy.

   _____   _____

7. The dessert is no place to eat your desert.

   _____   _____

8. Be careful not to loose your lose change.

   _____   _____

9. The angil was quit pretty.

   _____   _____

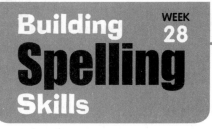

Spelling List

This Week's Focus:
- Spell words with the suffixes **-less**, **-ful**, and **-ness**
- Spell words with the ending **-ly**

STEP 1 Read and Spell	STEP 2 Copy and Spell	STEP 3 Cover and Spell

fold

1. hopeless
2. careless
3. homeless
4. tireless
5. hopeful
6. fearful
7. cheerful
8. careful
9. graceful
10. happily
11. friendly
12. angrily
13. swiftly
14. suddenly
15. darkness
16. goodness
17. sadness
18. kindness
19. _____
   bonus word
20. _____
   bonus word

Word Meaning

Fill in the blanks with spelling words.

1. You don't need to be _____ of the _____ gazelle.

2. It is never _____ to help the _____ find a place to sleep.

3. The mother was _____ not to step on her child's toes.

4. The store clerk was always _____ when greeting a customer.

5. I wish there was more _____ and _____ in the world.

6. To everyone's surprise, the sound _____ stopped.

7. I was _____ that I could visit my friend.

8. The deer ran _____ through the forest.

My Spelling Dictation

Write the sentences. Circle the spelling words.

1. _____

_____

_____

2. _____

_____

_____

Word Study

Add a suffix or ending to make spelling words.

> less   ful   ness   ly

1. hope   _hopeful_
2. hope   _____
3. sad   _____
4. friend   _____
5. tire   _____
6. fear   _____
7. cheer   _____
8. home   _____
9. grace   _____

10. happy   _____
11. care   _____
12. angry   _____
13. swift   _____
14. sudden   _____
15. dark   _____
16. good   _____
17. care   _____
18. kind   _____

Now circle the words above that required a change before adding the suffix or ending.

Divide these words into syllables.

1. hopeless   _____ _____
2. hopeful   _____ _____
3. darkness   _____ _____
4. angrily   _____ _____ _____
5. happily   _____ _____ _____

6. friendly   _____ _____
7. kindness   _____ _____

Edit for Spelling

Circle the 12 misspelled words below.
Write the words correctly on the lines.

There's Always Hope

Sudenly, there was darknes. I was carelass to let my flashlight

go out while camping in the backyard. I sat fearfull about the strange

noises coming from everywhere. I was hopefull I could find some

batteries. I was tireles in my search, but I finally gave up. All seemed

hopelass. Sadnuss filled my body.

When all seemed lost, a gracefil figure tiptoed up to my tent.

A friendy face peeked inside. My mom was cheerfal when she asked,

"Is everything all right out here?"

My worries vanished swifly, as my mom handed me a new

package of batteries.

_____   _____

_____   _____

_____   _____

_____   _____

_____   _____

_____   _____

Building Spelling Skills

WEEK 29

Spelling List

This Week's Focus:
- Spell words with the prefixes **dis-**, **un-**, **re-**, and **mis-**

STEP 1 Read and Spell	STEP 2 Copy and Spell	STEP 3 Cover and Spell

fold

1. disappear

2. disappoint

3. disagree

4. dishonest

5. unable

6. uncertain

7. unbeaten

8. uncomfortable

9. unkind

10. unknown

11. rewrite

12. review

13. rebuild

14. recall

15. misbehave

16. misuse

17. misunderstand

18. misspell

19. _____
   bonus word

20. _____
   bonus word

Word Meaning

Complete the crossword puzzle using spelling words.

Across

1. to make again
4. not known
5. uneasy
9. to look over again
10. not nice
11. to remember

Down

2. can't do
3. to argue
4. not sure
6. to spell wrong
7. to write again
8. to use incorrectly

My Spelling Dictation

Write the sentences. Circle the spelling words.

1. _____

   _____

   _____

2. _____

   _____

   _____

Word Study

Add the correct prefix to the base word.
Write the word in the blank.

> dis   un   re   mis

1. The child was unhappy because he was _____ to ride the horse.
   able

2. She couldn't _____ her friend's name.
   call

3. You may get hurt if you _____ that tool.
   use

4. I'm afraid I must _____ with your opinion.
   agree

5. Did you _____ that word? Check the dictionary.
   spell

6. Use nice paper to _____ your report.
   write

7. The runner was happy to announce that she was _____
   beaten
   in all of her races.

8. Because he was _____ his answer was correct, he thought
   certain
   about it again.

9. The rainbow will soon _____.
   appear

10. The princess thought the bed was _____.
    comfortable

Edit for Spelling

Circle the words that are spelled correctly.

disappear	disapoint	dishonest	uncomfortable
disagree	review	missbehave	mispell
unable	uncurtain	unknown	recall
unbeten	unkind	rebild	misunderstand

Circle the misspelled words in the sentences.
Write them correctly on the lines.

1. The magician didn't disapoint the audience. He made a rabbit disapear.

   _____ _____

2. Students can missunderstand the meaning of a word, especially
   when it is mispelled.

   _____ _____

3. I'm sure you won't disagre that it is bad to be dishonist.

   _____ _____

4. If I recal correctly, you often missbehave.

   _____ _____

5. Let's revew and rerite your notes so you will do better on the test.

   _____ _____

6. I always get uncomfortible when someone is being unkin.

   _____ _____

Spelling List

This Week's Focus:
• Spell multisyllabic words

STEP 1 Read and Spell	STEP 2 Copy and Spell	STEP 3 Cover and Spell

fold

1. multiply

2. imagination

3. favorite

4. computer

5. citizenship

6. invisible

7. undercover

8. enjoyment

9. discussion

10. America

11. unusual

12. example

13. melody

14. temperature

15. understanding

16. experiment

17. explanation

18. oxygen

19. _____
        bonus word

20. _____
        bonus word

Word Meaning

Fill in the blanks with spelling words.

1. We had to adjust the _____ because everyone was cold.

2. My _____ thing is to use my creativity and

   _____ to write a story.

3. I get so much _____ from my new _____.

4. Every person in the United States of _____ should practice

   good _____.

5. My _____ of the game was better the second time.

6. The clever _____ agent tried to make himself

   _____ in the crowd.

7. She played an _____ _____ on her guitar.

8. Finding the area of a square is an _____ of when to

   _____.

My Spelling Dictation

Write the sentences. Circle the spelling words.

1. _____

   _____

   _____

2. _____

   _____

   _____

Word Study

Write the spelling word that means the opposite
of each word or phrase.

1. least-liked _____

2. visible _____

3. divide _____

4. typical _____

Divide these words into syllables.

1. multiply _____ _____ _____

2. favorite _____ _____ _____

3. enjoyment _____ _____ _____

4. temperature _____ _____ _____ _____

5. oxygen _____ _____ _____

6. discussion _____ _____ _____

7. citizenship _____ _____ _____ _____

8. America _____ _____ _____ _____

9. unusual _____ _____ _____

10. understanding _____ _____ _____ _____

11. explanation _____ _____ _____ _____

12. imagination _____ _____ _____ _____ _____

Edit for Spelling

Circle the 14 misspelled words below.
Write the words correctly on the lines.

My Friend the Computer Programmer

My friend, the computor programmer, has a great imagenation. For exampel, he has created programs that

- help students learn to multipi,

- explain how to practice good citisenship,

- give facts about the United States of Amereca, and

- help students write songs for a cyber rock band.

My friend is now working on two programs, an unusal action game and a cyber science experiment. The action game will have an invisable undorcover police officer as the hero. The experement will help students with their undurstanding of oxigen and tempurature. He hopes both programs will bring injoyment to many students.

_____   _____

_____   _____

_____   _____

_____   _____

_____   _____

_____   _____

_____   _____

Note: Use this form to track students' spelling progress.

Spelling Record Sheet

Students' Names															
1															
2															
3															
4															
5															
6															
7															
8															
9															
10															
11															
12															
13															
14															
15															
16															
17															
18															
19															
20															
21															
22															
23															
24															
25															
26															
27															
28															
29															
30															

My Spelling Record

Building Spelling Skills

Spelling List	Date	Number Correct	Words Missed

Spelling Test

Building Spelling Skills

Listen to the words.
Write each word on a line.

1. _____   11. _____

2. _____   12. _____

3. _____   13. _____

4. _____   14. _____

5. _____   15. _____

6. _____   16. _____

7. _____   17. _____

8. _____   18. _____

9. _____   19. _____

10. _____   20. _____

Listen to the sentences.
Write them on the lines.

1. _____

_____

_____

2. _____

_____

_____

Building Spelling Skills

Spelling List

Note: Reproduce this form to make your own spelling list.

STEP 1 Read and Spell

fold

STEP 2 Copy and Spell

STEP 3 Cover and Spell

1. _____
2. _____
3. _____
4. _____
5. _____
6. _____
7. _____
8. _____
9. _____
10. _____
11. _____
12. _____
13. _____
14. _____
15. _____
16. _____
17. _____
18. _____
19. _____
20. _____

Building Spelling Skills, Daily Practice • EMC 2708

Crossword Puzzle

Across	Down

Building Spelling Skills

Dear Parents,

Attached is your child's spelling list for this week. Encourage him or her to practice the words in one or more of these ways:

1. Read and spell each word. Cover it up and write it. Uncover the word and check to see if it is correct.

2. Find the words on the spelling list in printed materials such as books and magazines.

3. Read a word aloud and ask your child to spell it (either aloud or written on paper).

Thank you for your support of our spelling program.

Sincerely,

Building Spelling Skills

Dear Parents,

Attached is your child's spelling list for this week. Encourage him or her to practice the words in one or more of these ways:

1. Read and spell each word. Cover it up and write it. Uncover the word and check to see if it is correct.

2. Find the words on the spelling list in printed materials such as books and magazines.

3. Read a word aloud and ask your child to spell it (either aloud or written on paper).

Thank you for your support of our spelling program.

Sincerely,

Student Spelling Dictionaries

Self-made spelling dictionaries provide students with a reference for the spelling of words they frequently use in their writing.

Materials

- copy of "My Own Spelling Dictionary" form (page 147)
- 26 sheets of lined paper—6" x 9" (15 x 23 cm)
- 2 sheets of construction paper or tagboard for cover—6" x 9" (15 x 23 cm)

- crayons or markers
- glue
- stapler
- masking tape

Steps to Follow

❶ Color and cut out the cover sheet form. Glue it to the front cover of the dictionary.

❷ Staple the lined paper inside the cover. Place masking tape over the staples.

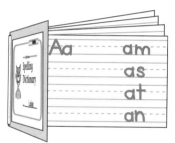

❸ Guide students (or ask parent volunteers) to write a letter of the alphabet on each page.

What to Include

1. When students ask for the correct spelling of a special word, have them write it in their dictionary.

2. Include special words being learned as part of science or social studies units.

3. Include words for special holidays.

4. Include the common words students continue to misspell on tests and in daily written work.

5. Add color and number words if these are not on charts posted in the classroom.

146

My Own
Spelling
Dictionary

Name _____

My Own
Spelling
Dictionary

Name _____

147

Master Word List

able	beautiful	clasp	didn't	false	happier
across	because	cleaner	disagree	families	happiest
action	began	cleanest	disappear	family	happily
address	believe	climate	disappoint	fasten	haven't
afternoon	between	climber	discussion	faucet	heard
again	bicycle	close	dishonest	fault	heaven
aisle	bigger	cloth	display	favorite	heavier
all ready	biggest	clothes	ditch	fearful	heaviest
almost	birthday	clues	ditches	February	herd
alone	blizzard	coach	divide	few	hero
alphabet	blush	collar	division	fiction	heroes
already	bottom	collide	doctor	fifteen	herself
also	bought	color	does	fifty	himself
America	bowl	compass	dollar	figure	holiday
among	breakfast	computer	don't	flashlight	homeless
amount	bridge	concert	doubt	flavor	hoped
angel	brighter	conclusion	doughnut	flight	hopeful
angle	brother	control	downstairs	flour	hopeless
angrily	brought	copy	draft	foe	hoping
ankle	burglar	cough	dragonfly	follow	hour
annoy	busier	could've	drown	forest	however
another	busiest	couldn't	duty	fought	human
answer	buy	cousin	eager	fountain	hungry
anyone	calendar	crawl	earlier	freedom	I'm
appear	calf	crowded	earliest	freight	imagination
appeared	cardinal	cruel	early	friendly	inch
appearing	careful	crunch	earth	frighten	invisible
applaud	careless	crutch	easy	front	island
appoint	cattle	cubicle	eclipse	fuel	isle
April	caught	curly	edge	future	isn't
aren't	caution	cute	educate	gather	it's
athlete	ceiling	cycle	education	gentle	item
attach	celebrate	cypress	else	geography	January
attend	cereal	dairy	empty	ghost	journey
attention	chalkboard	damage	enjoy	gigantic	journeys
attract	change	dancer	enjoyment	giraffe	judge
August	changed	dangerous	enough	given	July
autumn	changing	darkness	everything	glance	June
avoid	cheerful	daughter	example	gnawed	junior
awesome	chief	daydream	experiment	goodness	keyboard
awful	choice	decide	explain	graceful	kindness
awhile	choose	delight	explanation	grade	knelt
bakery	chute	describe	explode	grandparents	knock
banana	cinder	desert	express	gravity	later
barber	circle	dessert	expression	grumpy	laundry
battle	citizenship	diary	fact	halt	lawyer

lazier	none	racing	singer	thought	we're
laziest	November	rapid	sketch	thousand	weather
lazy	nowhere	rattled	skyscraper	thread	Wednesday
leaf	o'clock	rattling	slimy	throat	weigh
leaves	obey	really	slippery	through	when
ledge	occurrence	rebuild	smoky	Thursday	where
libraries	ocean	recall	sneakers	tighten	whether
library	October	receive	snowflake	tireless	which
lightning	office	recent	soft	title	whisper
listen	officer	refrigerator	somewhere	toast	whistle
lived	often	regular	southwest	too	who
living	ought	review	space	tougher	who's
loose	our	rewrite	spelling	traffic	whole
lose	outfield	right	spring	traveled	whose
magic	oxygen	roof	squeeze	traveling	why
magician	oyster	roofs	stalk	triangle	wild
main	paragraph	rougher	stall	trophy	wolf
matter	pedal	roughest	straight	trouble	wolves
mean	penny	ruin	strait	truth	wonder
medal	people	sadness	strange	Tuesday	world
meddle	pharmacy	sailor	stranger	twice	worse
melody	photograph	sandwich	string	twilight	worth
menu	phrase	Saturday	strong	two	wound
mighty	physician	saucer	studied	umpire	wrapped
million	piano	scarecrow	studying	unable	wrapper
mind	picnic	scent	suddenly	unbeaten	wrapping
minute	picture	schoolroom	sugar	uncertain	wreath
misbehave	piece	scissors	summer	uncle	wrench
mission	pilot	sealing	suppertime	uncomfortable	wrist
misspell	pitcher	search	surface	undercover	write
misunderstand	pollute	season	swiftly	understanding	wrong
misuse	pollution	second	switch	uniform	year
moisture	potato	secret	taught	unkind	you'll
month	potatoes	September	telephone	unknown	you're
mountain	prepare	service	temperature	unusual	
much	problem	shampoo	tenth	used	
multiply	program	shirt	that's	usual	
music	pronounce	shoes	their	vacant	
musician	pulley	shoot	then	vein	
naughty	puny	shower	there	village	
neighbor	purchase	shown	these	voice	
nephew	quicker	shrimp	they'd	volcano	
news	quickest	sight	they're	voyage	
nightly	quiet	sign	they've	walked	
nobody	quite	signal	thirsty	wallet	
noise	raced	since	thirty	watch	

Answer Key

Page 21
1. burglar, freedom
2. eclipse
3. snowflake
4. hungry, between
5. attract, twilight
6. glance, slimy
7. trouble, laundry

Page 22
1. burglar
2. glance
3. trouble
4. gravity
5. hungry
6. twilight
7. freedom
8. bridge
9. attract
10. between
11. snowflake
12. switch

glance
snowflake
trouble
eclipse
(freedom)
(between)
(secret)
bridge

1. hun — cret
2. se — gry
3. laun — ble
4. trou — light
5. twi — dry
6. be — dom
7. snow — flake
8. free — tween

1. hungry
2. secret
3. laundry
4. trouble
5. twilight
6. between
7. snowflake
8. freedom

Page 23
These words should be circled:
1. freedom
2. between
3. twilight
4. attract
5. trouble
6. applaud
7. bridge
8. secret

These words should be circled and written correctly:
1. (glanc) glance
   (hugry) hungry
2. (swich) switch
   (lawndry) laundry
3. (dascribe) describe
   (slimee) slimy
4. (Gravety) Gravity
   (snoflak) snowflake
5. (burgler) burglar
   (eclips) eclipse

Page 25
1. where, spring
2. athlete, awhile
3. whistle, gather
4. watch, these
5. change, sandwich
6. singer, whisper
7. thirsty, nowhere
8. worth, slippery

Page 26
1. (these)   ga(th)er   (th)read
   a(th)lete   wor(th)   (th)irsty
2. atta(ch)   (ch)ange   sandwi(ch)
3. wat(ch)
4. where   whisper   whistle
   awhile   nowhere

1. nowhere
2. thirsty
3. watch
4. where
5. attach
6. awhile
7. worth
8. gather
9. change
10. these
11. thread
12. whisper
13. sandwich
14. athlete
15. whistle

Page 27
These words should be underlined:
slippery, worth, spring, nowhere, whistle

These words should be circled and written correctly:
1. (Atach)   Attach
   (Sandwech)   sandwich
2. (athle)   athlete
   (thirsdy)   thirsty
3. (wached)   watched
   (singr)   singer
4. (whispor)   whisper
   (awile)   awhile
5. (No where)   Nowhere
   (wurth)   worth
6. (whistel)   whistle
   (changs)   changes

Page 29
1. grade
2. neighbor, April
3. stranger
4. explain
5. ankle, able
6. weigh
7. display
8. space

Page 30
long **a** sound
expl(ai)n   (a)ble   l(a)ter   sp(a)ce
str(a)nger gr(a)de displ(ay) m(ai)n
n(ei)ghbor w(ei)gh v(ei)n   (A)pril
fr(ei)ght

short **a** sound
f(a)ct beg(a)n cl(a)sp r(a)pid (a)nkle

1. neigh — play
2. dis — bor
3. be — ger
4. ex — id
5. stran — gan
6. rap — plain

1. neighbor
2. display
3. began
4. explain
5. stranger
6. rapid

Page 31
These words should be circled and written correctly:
display, space, began, facts, explained, weigh, rapid, stranger, main, freight, April's, grade, later, neighbor, neighbor

Page 33
1. squeeze, piece
2. else, people
3. fifteen, tenth
4. spelling, believe
5. empty, mean
6. eager, sketch
7. easy, sneakers
8. When, receive

Page 34
1. squ(ee)ze
2. else
3. bel(ie)ve
4. when
5. tenth
6. sn(ea)kers
7. sketch
8. (ea)sy
9. (ea)ger
10. empt(y)
11. m(ea)n
12. fift(ee)n
13. rec(ei)ve
14. p(ie)ce
15. edge
16. spelling
17. p(eo)ple
18. then

1. wh(e)n
2. mean
3. believe
4. piece
5. (e)mpty
6. (e)dge
7. sk(e)tch
8. sp(e)lling
9. receive
10. t(e)nth
11. (e)lse
12. fifteen
13. eager
14. squeeze
15. sneakers
16. easy
17. people
18. th(e)n

believe receive piece

1. squeeze   6. mean
2. eager   7. believe
3. piece   8. sketch
4. empty   9. edge
5. receive   10. easy

Page 35
These words should be circled:
1. believe   7. empty
2. piece   8. mean
3. receive   9. squeeze
4. else   10. spelling
5. easy   11. people
6. sketch   12. eager

These words should be circled
and written correctly:
1. (tanth)   tenth
   (fifeteen)   fifteen
   (peple)   people
2. (sneekers)   sneakers
   (Than)   Then
3. (Whin)   When
4. (els)   else
   (edg)   edge

Page 37
Down
1. buy
2. title
3. which
5. string
6. picnic
9. wild

Across
3. why
4. inch
5. skyscraper
7. decide
8. since
9. write
10. right

Page 38
fix
since
which
inch
string
shrimp
picnic
bicycle

pie
title
mind
wild
decide
why
skyscraper
buy
right
lightning
write
cypress
bicycle

1. ti — cide   1. title
2. pic — ning   2. picnic
3. de — tle   3. decide
4. light — nic   4. lightning
5. cy — press   5. cypress

Page 39
1. since
2. write
3. string
4. title

These words should be circled
and written correctly:
picnic, wild, Why, bicycle, lightning,
inch, decide, which, shrimp,
skyscraper, cypress

Page 41
1. a. strong   e. problem
   b. whole   f. wrong
   c. control   g. bottom
   d. copy   h. foe
2. a. October
   b. bowl
   c. doughnut
   d. toast
   e. cloth
   f. throat
   g. coach

Page 42

fox	goat
strong	foe
wrong	doughnut
copy	toast
cloth	coach
problem	throat
bottom	smoky
	whole
	explode
	shown
	bowl

(wrong) (whole) shown bowl
explode doughnut foe throat

Page 43
These words should be circled
and written correctly:
1. (donat)   doughnut
   (octobr)   October
2. (rong)   wrong
   (strang)   strong
3. (Copee)   Copy
   (probelm)   problem
4. (shoan)   shown
   (boal)   bowl
5. (coch)   coach
   (smokey)   smoky
6. (fo)   foe

7. (tost)   toast
   (throt)   throat
8. (hole)   whole
   (battom)   bottom
9. (explod)   explode

Page 45
1. c   10. o
2. n   11. l
3. a   12. m
4. b   13. f
5. h   14. g
6. i   15. j
7. d
8. e
9. k

Page 46

cup	use
blush	uniform
crutch	usual
crunch	human
grumpy	cubicle
much	cute
uncle	fuel
umpire	used
none	
does	

1. grum—ture   1. grumpy
2. um—man   2. umpire
3. hu—cle   3. human
4. un—pire   4. uncle
5. fu—py   5. future
6. beau—u—ful   6. beautiful
7. un—i—al   7. uniform
8. us—i—cle   8. usual
9. cub—ti—form   9. cubicle

Page 47
These words should be circled and
written correctly:
uncle, uniform, cute, fuel, none,
umpire, grumpy, beautiful, crunch,
blush, crutch, much

Page 49
Down
1. office
3. address
4. follow
6. matter
8. million
10. penny

Across
2. village
5. occurrence
7. summer
9. dollars
11. wallet
12. wrapper

Page 50

1. address
2. blizzard
3. wallet
4. collide
5. office
6. wrapper
7. penny
8. million
9. village
10. battle
11. follow
12. scissors
13. matter
14. summer
15. cattle
16. dollar
17. suppertime
18. occurrence

1. fol — low
2. bat — tle
3. mat — ter
4. col — lide
5. of — fice
6. cat — tle
7. vil — lage
8. wal — let
9. pen — ny
10. scis — sors
11. dol — lar
12. mil — lion

1. follow
2. battle
3. matter
4. collide
5. office
6. cattle
7. village
8. wallet
9. penny
10. scissors
11. dollar
12. million

Page 51

These words should be circled:
dollar village collide cattle suppertime million summer

These words should be circled and written correctly:

1. ofice — office
   villag — village
2. addres — address
   Sumer — Summer
3. folow — follow
   scisors — scissors
4. dollers — dollars
   pennie — penny
5. blizzerd — blizzard
   millon — million
6. cattle — cattle
   battle — battle

Page 53

1. a. January e. July
   b. August f. November
   c. February
   d. September
2. a. Tuesday c. Wednesday
   b. Thursday d. Saturday
3. a year
4. a month

1. seasons   2. calendar

Page 54

1. c
2. a
3. b
4. g
5. f
6. e
7. d

1. f
2. c
3. i
4. g
5. h
6. j
7. l
8. k
9. d
10. a
11. e
12. b

Page 55

These words should be circled:
September, holiday, year, month, Tuesday, July, February, second, Wednesday

These words should be circled and written correctly:

1. holeday — holiday
   Wednsday — Wednesday
2. mounth — month
   Janary — January
3. mintes — minutes
   seconts — seconds
4. Tusday — Tuesday
   Thersday — Thursday
5. Juli — July
6. Satarday — Saturday

Page 57

1. purchase, banana
2. compass, ocean
3. pedal, across
4. mountain
5. alone
6. often
7. given, color
8. brother, cousin

9. appear, front
10. again

Page 58

across alone among again
about appear brother banana
compass heaven mountain ocean
cousin given often

1. a cross
2. a lone
3. a mong
4. a gain
5. ap pear
6. moun tain
7. broth er
8. com pass
9. ba na na
10. giv en
11. heav en
12. o cean
13. cous in
14. pur chase
15. of ten
16. col or
17. ped al

Page 59

These words should be circled:
1. heaven
2. ocean
3. color
4. pedal
5. appear
6. again
7. banana
8. front

These words should be circled and written correctly:

1. cousan brothur acros mowntens
   cousin brother across mountains
2. pruchased compas amung
   purchased compass among
3. alon
   alone
4. ofton givan
   often given

Page 61

1. I'm
2. don't, o'clock
3. who's
4. aren't
5. isn't
6. Didn't
7. It's
8. We're
9. You're

Page 62

1. aren't o
2. don't o
3. you'll wi
4. they've ha
5. could've ha

6. they'd   woul
7. who's   i
8. it's   i
9. I'm   a
10. isn't   o
11. we're   a
12. o'clock   f the
13. haven't   o
14. couldn't   o
15. you're   a
16. they're   a
17. that's   i
18. didn't   o

Page 63
1. I'm
2. it's
3. who's
4. they'd
5. could've
6. they've
7. you'll
8. don't
9. aren't
10. isn't
11. we're
12. o'clock
13. haven't
14. couldn't
15. you're
16. that's
17. they're
18. didn't

These words should be circled and written correctly:
1. doen't — don't
   Thay're — They're
   o'clock — o'clock
2. Who'se — Who's
   doen't — don't
3. You'r — You're
   Were — We're
4. Thats — That's
   Im — I'm
   You'l — You'll
5. Its — It's

Page 65
Down
1. outfield
2. breakfast
3. birthday
5. dragonfly
6. daydream
7. keyboard

Across
4. himself
8. grandparent
9. nobody
10. anyone
11. scarecrow

Page 66
1. chalkboard
2. somewhere
3. afternoon
4. however
5. herself
6. grandparents

1. any/one
2. how/ever
3. every/thing
4. him/self
5. birth/day
6. her/self
7. some/where
8. after/noon
9. chalk/board
10. day/dream
11. down/stairs
12. grand/parents
13. break/fast
14. out/field
15. scare/crow
16. no/body
17. dragon/fly
18. key/board

Page 67
These words should be circled and written correctly:
1. any one — anyone
   birth day — birthday
2. her self — herself
   hemself — himself
3. every thing — everything
   dragon fly — dragonfly
4. Somwhere — Somewhere
   key borad — keyboard
5. outfeild — outfield
   chalk board — chalkboard
6. No body — Nobody
   scarcrow — scarecrow
7. grandparants — grandparents
   break fast — breakfast
8. day dreaming — daydreaming
   down stairs — downstairs

These words should be circled:
1. outfield
2. afternoon
3. everything
4. breakfast
5. nobody

Page 69
Three of the following should be written:
1. living   rattling   studying
   traveling   changing   appearing
   racing   hoping   wrapping

Three of the following should be written:
2. lived   rattled   studied
   traveled   changed   appeared
   raced   hoped   wrapped
3. a. travel   e. live
   b. study   f. hope
   c. race   g. rattle
   d. change   h. appear

Page 70
1. living - drop **e**
2. wrapping - double final consonant
3. rattling - drop **e**
4. hoping - drop **e**
5. studying - no change
6. racing - drop **e**
7. traveling - no change
8. changing - drop **e**
9. appearing - no change

1. lived - drop **e**
2. wrapped - double final consonant
3. rattled - drop **e**
4. hoped - drop **e**
5. studied - change **y** to **i**
6. raced - drop **e**
7. traveled - no change
8. changed - drop **e**
9. appeared - no change

Page 71
1. rattling
2. racing
3. traveled
4. changing
5. appearing

These words should be circled and written correctly:
traveling   raced   studied
changed   wrapping   lived
appeared   hoped

Page 73
Down
1. lazier
2. busiest
3. bigger
5. rougher
7. cleaner
8. earlier

Across
4. biggest
6. roughest
7. cleanest
9. earliest
10. heavier

Page 74
1. cleaner - no change
2. bigger - double final consonant
3. earlier - change **y** to **i**
4. quicker - no change
5. busier - change **y** to **i**
6. rougher - no change
7. heavier - change **y** to **i**
8. happier - change **y** to **i**
9. lazier - change **y** to **i**

1. cleanest - no change
2. biggest - double final consonant
3. earliest - change **y** to **i**
4. quickest - no change
5. busiest - change **y** to **i**
6. roughest - no change
7. heaviest - change **y** to **i**
8. happiest - change **y** to **i**
9. laziest - change **y** to **i**

Page 75
These words should be circled:

heaviest   quick
lazy   quicker
busy   cleanest
roughest   happiest

These words should be circled and written correctly:

1. biggest   bigger
2. earlest   earliest
3. lazier   laziest
4. happyer   happier
5. heaviesr   heavier
6. busyes   busiest
7. quickies   quickest
8. cleaniest   cleanest
9. roughor   rougher
10. hapiest   happiest
11. busyer   busier

Page 77
1. shirt, collar
2. worse, world
3. sailor, doctor
4. barber, curly
5. earth, shower
6. service, wonder, bakery
7. early, another
8. thirty, surface

Page 78
1. doctor
2. barber
3. shower
4. wonder
5. sailor
6. another
7. dollar
8. service
9. worse
10. bakery
11. world
12. thirty
13. curly
14. shirt

1. ear ly
2. thir ty
3. doc tor
4. ser vice
5. won der
6. bar ber
7. sur face
8. cur ly
9. sail or
10. show er
11. dol lar
12. col lar

Page 79
These words should be circled and written correctly:

thirty   Earth   world   shower
surface   service   doctor
worse   early   search   sailor   curly

Page 81

Down
1. journeys
2. leaf
3. hero
6. leaves
7. ditches
8. ditch
9. roofs
12. potato

Across
4. wolves
5. journey
10. families
11. wolf
13. heroes
14. potatoes
15. roof

Page 82
1. leaves - change **f** to **v**, add **es**
2. heroes - add **es**
3. potatoes - add **es**
4. families - change **y** to **i**, add **es**
5. ditches - add **es**
6. wolves - change **f** to **v**, add **es**
7. libraries - change **y** to **i**, add **es**
8. journeys - add **s**

1. he roes
2. ditch es
3. jour neys
4. po ta toes
5. fam i lies
6. li brar ies

Page 83
These words should be circled:

libraries   potatoes   ditches
wolves

These words should be circled and written correctly:

1. famile   family
    ditchs   ditches
2. herow   hero
    potatos   potatoes
3. leafs   leaves
    rooves   roofs
4. wolfs   wolves
    journy   journey
5. familes   families
    librare   library
6. rouf   roof
7. woolf   wolf
    leef   leaf
8. heros   heroes
    libraryes   libraries

Page 85
1. a. also
   b. crawl
   c. false
   d. soft
2. a. soft
   b. halt
   c. false
   d. bought
3. a. officer   e. cough
   b. faucet   f. because
   c. saucer   g. also
   d. lawyer   h. crawl

Page 86

fall	caught	law
also	faucet	lawyer
almost	saucer	awesome
false	caution	crawl
stalk	because	awful
halt		
stall		

loft	trough
officer	bought
soft	cough

1. be — some   1. because
2. awe — cause   2. awesome
3. al — cet   3. also
4. law — so   4. lawyer
5. fau — yer   5. faucet
6. sau — tion   6. saucer
7. cau — most   7. caution
8. al — cer   8. almost

Page 87
These words should be circled:
almost, cough, lawyer, faucet, stalk, bought, stall, awful, awesome, saucer

These words should be circled and written correctly:

1. all most   almost
    sawcer   saucer
2. layer   lawyer
    cawtion   caution
3. awsome   awesome
    crall   crawl
4. baht   bought
    saft   soft
5. auful   awful
    cauf   cough

6. (faucet) faucet
   (becauze) because
7. (offisor) officer
   (Halt) Halt
8. (allso) also
   (fallse) false

Page 89
dancer strange dangerous
circle cardinal gentle damage

cereal sugar signal regular
concert

Page 90

soft **c**	hard **c**
cinder	circle
circle	cardinal
concert	concert
cereal	cycle
cycle	
dancer	
celebrate	
twice	

soft **g**	hard **g**
dangerous	signal
strange	regular
ledge	sugar
damage	geography
geography	
gentle	

1. cycle   5. signal
2. circle   6. gentle
3. celebrate   7. strange
4. geography   8. dangerous

1. damage   3. strange
2. dangerous   4. gentle

Page 91
These words should be circled:
strange cinder ledge sugar
cycle cardinal regular
dangerous

These words should be circled
and written correctly:
1. (dansir)   dancer
   (twise)   twice
2. (cardinel) cardinal
   (ceriol)   cereal
3. (dangerus) dangerous
   (lege)   ledge

Page 92
4. (geograpy) geography
   (strang)   strange
5. (reguler)   regular
   (sinder)   cinder
6. (damege)   damage
   (signel)   signal

Page 93
Down   **Across**
1. clues   3. duty
2. few   4. cruel
5. ruin   6. news
7. whose   9. conclusion
8. June   10. shoes
9. choose   11. who
11. wound   12. schoolroom

Page 94
1. few   10. ruin
2. schoolroom   11. through
3. June   12. news
4. cruel   13. whose
5. shoes   14. conclusion
6. truth   15. shampoo
7. duty   16. wound
8. who   17. clues
9. choose   18. junior

1. 1   10. 1
2. 1   11. 2
3. 1   12. 1
4. 2   13. 3
5. 1   14. 1
6. 2   15. 2
7. 1   16. 2
8. 1   17. 1
9. 1   18. 2

Page 95
These words should be circled
and written correctly:
schoolroom duty News through
few clues conclusion truth
wounded Who cruel junior June
whose

Page 97
crowded voice noise
appoint amount

voyage thousand
southwest(ern) pronounce
oyster flour choice enjoy

Page 98
1. (voice)   6. a(voi)d
2. (oyster)   7. app(oin)t
3. v(oya)ge   8. en(joy)
4. ann(oy)   9. m(oi)sture
5. ch(oi)ce   10. n(oi)se

1. dr(ow)n   5. s(ou)thwest
2. am(ou)nt   6. th(ou)sand
3. f(ou)ntain   7. fl(ou)r
4. cr(ow)ded   8. pron(ou)nce

1. oys ——— nounce   1. oyster
2. an ——— ter   2. annoy
3. pro ——— tain   3. pronounce
4. foun ——— noy   4. fountain
5. a ——— mount   5. amount
6. thou ——— ture   6. thousand
7. south ——— sand   7. southwest
8. mois ——— west   8. moisture
9. en ——— age   9. enjoy
10. voy ——— joy   10. voyage

Page 99
These words should be circled:
1. amount   5. voice
2. thousand   6. appoint
3. enjoy   7. pronounce
4. voyage   8. southwest

These words should be circled
and written correctly:
1. (anoy)   annoy
   (noice)   noise
2. (avoed)   avoid
   (droun)   drown
3. (choece)   choice
   (oister)   oyster
4. (flowr)   flour
5. (crouded)   crowded
6. (moistur)   moisture

Page 101
Across   **Down**
1. phrase   1. photograph
2. enough   3. nephew
4. chief   5. fifty
7. paragraph   6. trophy
10. pharmacy   8. alphabet
11. telephone   9. draft

Page 102

1. enough
2. tougher
3. fifty
4. pharmacy
5. alphabet
6. nephew
7. trophy
8. paragraph
9. telephone
10. photograph
11. giraffe
12. forest
13. figure
14. refrigerator
15. draft
16. phrase
17. traffic
18. chief

1. figure
2. giraffe
3. fifty
4. traffic
5. draft
6. alphabet
7. paragraph
8. trophy
9. chief
10. phrase
11. refrigerator
12. pharmacy
13. enough
14. forest
15. photograph
16. telephone
17. nephew
18. tougher

Page 103

These words should be circled and written correctly:

Pharmacy nephew fifty tougher enough forest giraffes nephew trophy photograph paragraph chief

Page 105

daughter thought brought nightly frighten flight flashlight caught sight brighter brighter delight naughty daughter

Page 106

1. flight
2. delight
3. thought
4. caught
5. bright or brought
6. brought or bright

1. brought
2. fault
3. thought
4. fought
5. caught
6. daughter
7. taught
8. naughty

1. frighten
2. flight
3. brighter
4. flashlight
5. mighty
6. delight
7. tighten
8. nightly

letters are g h

Page 107

These words should be circled:
caught delight taught ought sight

These words should be circled and written correctly:

1. ought — ought
   tighton — tighten
2. fallt — fault
   fouht — fought
3. cought — caught
   flit — flight
4. daughtor — daughter
   taght — taught
5. flashlite — flashlight
   nitly — nightly
6. sieght — sight
   trihten — frighten
7. thoug — thought
   naghty — naughty
8. broght — brought
   deliht — delight
9. brihter — brighter

Page 109

Down
1. knelt
2. fasten
3. answer
4. wreath
5. calf
6. island
10. climber
11. key
12. chin
14. judge

Across
4. wrench
7. scent
8. listen
9. eat
11. knock
13. walked
15. sign
16. doubt
17. wrist

Non-spelling words: eat, key, chin

Page 110

1. calf
2. walked
3. ghost
4. gnawed
5. climber
6. wreath
7. listen
8. island
9. scent
10. wrench
11. judge
12. fasten
13. wrist
14. doubt
15. knock
16. answer
17. knelt
18. sign

1. knelt
2. knock
3. wrist
4. wrench
5. wreath
6. gnawed
7. sign
8. calf
9. walked
10. climber
11. listen
12. fasten
13. answer
14. doubt
15. judge
16. scent

1. walked
2. fasten
3. ghost
4. gnawed
5. listen
6. answer

Page 111

1. wrench
2. wreath
3. walked
4. gnawed
5. knock
6. answer
7. doubt
8. wrist
9. judge
10. climber

1. lisson — Listen
   nock — knock
2. caf — calf
   nelt — knelt
3. dout — doubt
   sing — sign
4. juge — judge
   anser — answer
5. climer — climber
   fason — fasten
6. iland — island
   cent — scent
7. wist — wrist
   waked — walked
8. rench — wrench
   reath — wreath

Page 113

1. physician
2. magician
3. musician
4. attention
5. education
6. pollution
7. division
8. fiction
9. action
10. expression

1. pollute
2. divide
3. fiction
4. action

Page 114

1. expression
2. action
3. attention
4. division
5. education
6. pollution

two-syllable words	three-syllable words
action	division
fiction	attention
mission	pollution
divide	expression
attend	educate
pollute	musician
express	magician
music	physician
magic	

four-syllable words
education

Page 115
These words should be circled
and written correctly:
musician magician physician
musician music expression
physician musician attention
magician express physician
pollution magician divide
physician mission musician
magician physician

Page 117
1. pilot, volcano
2. climate, lazy
3. piano, program
4. flavor, menu
5. gigantic, pulley
6. prepare
7. recent, really
8. puny, obey
9. vacant, triangle

Page 118
All words should be underlined.
1. lazy   10. climate
2. volcano   11. gigantic
3. flavor   12. program
4. piano   13. obey
5. recent   14. puny
6. really   15. prepare
7. item   16. vacant
8. pilot   17. pulley
9. triangle   18. menu

lazy   item   really gigantic
flavor obey   piano   triangle

lazy   climate   recent
obey   menu   item

Page 119
These words should be circled:
climate recent pilot puny
obey program volcano

These words should be circled
and written correctly:
1. lasy   lazy
   vakint   vacant
2. itam   item
   valcano   volcano
3. flaver   flavor
   Gigantac   Gigantic
4. pielot   pilot
   realle   really
5. resent   recent
   pieno   piano

6. oby   obey
   puley   pulley
7. punee   puny
   menue   menu
8. climat   climate
   Triangel   Triangle
9. pripar   prepare
   programe   program

Page 121
Down   **Across**
1. too   2. shoot
3. their   5. straight
4. chute   6. strait
5. sealing   8. herd
7. medal   9. ceiling
8. heard   10. hour
9. close   12. there
11. our
12. two

Page 122
1. herd   6. shoot
2. close   7. ceiling
3. our   8. too
4. meddle   9. there
5. straight

1. there, their
2. hour, our
3. shoot, chute
4. two, too
5. strait, straight
6. meddle, medal
7. ceiling, sealing
8. our, hour
9. close, clothes

Page 123
These words should be circled
and written correctly:
our There hour shoot two
straight heard ceiling too close
herd sealing their medal

Page 125
1. quiet, quite
2. angel, angle
3. already, all ready
4. dessert, desert
5. whether, weather
6. pitcher, picture
7. loose, lose
8. aisle, isle
9. diary, dairy

Page 126
1. quiet   6. picture
2. angle   7. loose
3. already   8. aisle
4. desert   9. diary
5. weather

1. al —— gel   1. already
2. pit —— cher   2. pitcher
3. des —— er   3. desert
4. an —— ready   4. angel
5. wheth —— ert   5. whether
6. weath —— er   6. weather
7. qui —— sert   7. quiet
8. an —— et   8. angle
9. des —— gle   9. dessert

Page 127
These words should be circled:
dairy angle quite picture
already whether lose dessert
loose isle

These words should be circled
and written correctly:
1. aile   aisle
2. wheather   weather
   weather   whether
3. pitchor   pitcher
   pictur   picture
4. daire   dairy
   all read   all ready
5. quit   quiet
   diarry   diary
6. angal   angle
   alredy   already
7. dessert   desert
   desert   dessert
8. loose   lose
   lose   loose
9. angil   angel
   quit   quite

Page 129
1. fearful, graceful or friendly
2. hopeless, homeless
3. careful
4. friendly or cheerful
5. goodness, kindness OR
   kindness, goodness
6. suddenly
7. hopeful
8. swiftly

Page 130
1. hopeless or hopeful
2. hopeful or hopeless
3. sadness
4. friendly
5. tireless
6. fearful
7. cheerful
8. homeless
9. graceful
10. happily
11. careless or careful
12. angrily
13. swiftly
14. suddenly
15. darkness
16. goodness
17. careful or careless
18. kindness

1. hope less
2. hope ful
3. dark ness
4. an gri ly
5. hap pi ly
6. friend ly
7. kind ness

Page 131
These words should be circled and written correctly:
Suddenly darkness careless
fearful hopeful tireless hopeless
Sadness graceful friendly
cheerful swiftly

Page 133

Across	Down
1. rebuild	2. unable
4. unknown	3. disagree
5. uncomfortable	4. uncertain
9. review	6. misspell
10. unkind	7. rewrite
11. recall	8. misuse

Page 134
1. unable
2. recall
3. misuse
4. disagree
5. misspell
6. rewrite
7. unbeaten
8. uncertain
9. disappear
10. uncomfortable

Page 135
These words should be circled:
disappear, dishonest,
uncomfortable, disagree, review,
unable, unknown, recall, unkind,
misunderstand

These words should be circled and written correctly:
1. disapoint — disappoint
   disapear — disappear
2. missunderstand — misunderstand
   mispelled — misspelled
3. disagre — disagree
   dishonist — dishonest
4. recal — recall
   missbehave — misbehave
5. revew — review
   rerite — rewrite
6. uncomfortible — uncomfortable
   unkin — unkind

Page 137
1. temperature
2. favorite, imagination
3. enjoyment, computer
4. America, citizenship
5. understanding
6. undercover, invisible
7. unusual, melody
8. example, multiply

Page 138
1. favorite   3. multiply
2. invisible   4. unusual

1. mul ti ply
2. fa vor ite
3. en joy ment
4. tem per a ture
5. ox y gen
6. dis cus sion
7. cit i zen ship
8. A mer i ca
9. un us u al
10. un der stand ing
11. ex pla na tion
12. i mag i na tion

Page 139
These words should be circled and written correctly:
computer   imagination   example
multiply   citizenship   America
unusual   invisible   undercover
experiment   understanding
oxygen   temperature   enjoyment

Building Spelling Skills, Daily Practice • EMC 2708

NEW!

Daily Academic Vocabulary

Daily Academic Vocabulary, the newest addition to Evan-Moor's popular "Dailies" titles, is a supplemental vocabulary series for grades 2–6. This series features direct instruction of vocabulary, shown to be the most effective way to expand students' vocabulary. Both reproducible teacher's edition and student practice book formats are available.

Two Great Formats!

Reproducible Teacher's Edition

• Definitions and sample sentences for each week's words

• Ideas for how to introduce the words

• Instruction that builds on students' personal connection to the words

• 32 Transparencies that display each week's words, definitions, and sample sentences

Student Practice Books

• **Days 1–4** each week present three or four practice items that focus on using the words in a scholastic or personal context.

• **Day 5** is a review that features four multiple-choice items and an opened-ended writing activity that requires students to apply the words to their own experiences.

• **Four quarterly review weeks** give students additional practice on the words introduced in the prior eight weeks. Practice formats include cloze paragraphs, crosswords, and crack-the-code puzzles.

NEW!

Teacher's Edition		Student Pack (5 Student Books)	
Grade 2	EMC 2758 978-1-59673-201-8	Grade 2	EMC 6507 978-1-59673-208-7
Grade 3	EMC 2759 978-1-59673-202-5	Grade 3	EMC 6508 978-1-59673-209-4
Grade 4	EMC 2760 978-1-59673-203-2	Grade 4	EMC 6509 978-1-59673-210-0
Grade 5	EMC 2761 978-1-59673-204-9	Grade 5	EMC 6510 978-1-59673-211-7
Grade 6	EMC 2762 978-1-59673-205-6	Grade 6	EMC 6511 978-1-59673-212-4